super

ROOM MAKEOVER

Clive Gifford with Jane McAdam

Illustrated by David Graham
Cartoons by Tim Benton
Consultant: Kate Brookes

Hodder
Children's
Books

a division of Hodder Headline Limited

Text copyright 2000 © Clive Gifford and Jane McAdam
Illustration copyright 2000 © David Graham and Tim Benton
Published by Hodder Childrens Books 2000

Editor: Lyn Coutts
Series designed by Fiona Webb
Book designed by Joy Mutter, Picture Graphics

Tim Benton's cartoons can be found on the following pages: 1, 6-9, 12-15, 16 (top), 28, 38 (top), 42, 56, 70-71, 86-87, 98, 104 (top), 106, 110 (top), 112, 113 (top), 114 (top), and 117.

The right of Clive Gifford, Jane McAdam, David Graham and Tim Benton to be identified as the authors and illustrators of the work has been asserted by them in accordance with the Copyright, Designs and Patents Act 1988.

10 9 8 7 6 5 4 3 2 1

A catalogue record for this book is available from the British Library.

ISBN: 0 340 76469 4

All rights reserved. No part of this publication may be reproduced, stored in a retrieval system, or transmitted, in any form or by any means, without the prior written permission of the publisher, nor be otherwise circulated in any form of binding or cover other than that in which it is published and without a similar condition being imposed on the subsequent purchaser.

The information in this book has been thoroughly researched and checked for accuracy, and safety advice is given where appropriate. Neither the authors nor the publishers can accept any responsibility for any loss, injury or damage incurred as a result of using this book.

Printed by Clays Ltd, St Ives plc.

Hodder Children's Books
a division of Hodder Headline Limited
338 Euston Road
London NW1 3BH

Meet the author

Lumbered with the pink box room in the family home, nine-year-old Clive sulked and made not fair-type mutterings every time he passed his kid sister's bedroom. Sue, you see, had been given the big bedroom with a sweeping view across the fields. But after encouragement from his parents, Clive stopped muttering and started painting, hammering and being generally creative. His bedroom revamp on a jungle theme was so successful that his sister wanted to do a swap!

Many years and different rented rooms later, Clive is still painting, hammering and tinkering, but now in a proper workshop. His room improvement efforts have received a massive boost now that Clive's wife, Jane, who has real interior design skills, is part of the team. Jane helps sort out which ideas are really practical and which are not. (Jane recently rejected Clive's idea for turning their lounge into a scale model of Loftus Road, home of Clive's beloved football team, QPR.)

When the lid has been replaced on the paint tin and the brushes thoroughly washed, Clive takes a seat in front of his computer screen and indulges in his greatest pleasure – writing books for kids! *Room Makeover* is Clive's 42nd book.

Introduction

Mum and Dad had expected a girl, so when they brought home a baby boy they realised that the pink, flowery nursery that they had so lovingly prepared could be a problem. But being busy parents, there was never time to repaint and remove the frilly trimmings. It was not until I started visiting friends' homes and seeing their bedrooms that I understood that pink was not popular with the other boys in class 3A.

The only thing for it was to fix it, and fast. Sooner or later, my friends would want to come to my house, and I had my Tarzan-of-the-playground reputation to protect. With help and advice and free access to Dad's workshop and the treasure trove of bits and pieces it contained, I got to work removing every trace of pink, and every frill, flounce and flower. Then, I set about planning ways to make my small room lighter, brighter, less full of clutter and a lot more interesting.

The most important thing I learned then and with every room makeover since, is that it's often the smallest and simplest things that make the most difference.

This book won't tell you how to lay a concrete floor or plaster a wall, but it does show you how to work with what you've got and what is easily available. All it takes to turn tat into treasure is some thought, time and a few simple techniques. Let's get revamping!

Contents

1	Banish room gloom	6
2	Let's get started	16
3	It's a material world	28
4	Designs on sport	42
5	Computer crazy	56
6	The great outdoors . . . indoors!	70
7	Fright night	86
8	Top secret	98
9	Super solutions	106
	Want to know more?	118
	Glossary	121
	Index	125

 Banish room gloom

What is your room? The place where you sleep, store most of your stuff and get dressed and undressed? Certainly. Is it also where you study, chill out, read or listen to music? Probably. Chances are you also surf the Net and kick about with friends in your room. What's more, your room is where you should feel most happy, secure and relaxed. When looked at in this way, you expect an awful lot from four walls, floor and ceiling.

Is your room on top of its massive responsibilities or creaking under the strain? Would you like it to work even harder so that it will cope with your changing needs, your personality and your collection of rollerblades and skateboards? Whatever your frustration with your room, you've picked up the right book.

Mission possible

This book has two missions. The first is to fill you with makeover inspiration. The second is to explain and show you the nuts and bolts of how inspiration becomes a real object – something to look at, sit on or store stuff in. There are ideas that will make your friends green with envy or scare them witless (see Chapter 7, Fright night).

Despite what some interior designers say, it is perfectly possible to make great improvements to a room without robbing a bank. Many of the bits you'll need, you or your family will already have, some you will get for no cash outlay at all and others can be bought inexpensively.

You can do the bulk of the creative and manual work, though you may wisely ask an adult for advice. There are some jobs that will require adult help in the finishing-off stage. Adults can get very sensitive about bricks and mortar, so they would prefer to be involved when it comes to fixing hooks in a wall, for example.

This book needs you as much as you need the makeover tips and hints that this book offers. You've got to sit down, have a big think and identify what's good about your room and what is not so good (see pages 8-9). You need to spend time collecting materials and equipment, and planning and experimenting. Accept that every now and then, an idea may not turn out as expected or when completed, may look less cool than you would like, but most will look absolutely fabulous!

Banish room gloom

Does your room measure up?

Have a look at this room. Do any of its problems and drawbacks remind you of your pad?

Lack of storage

Curtains that just aren't you

Desk straining under the weight of accumulated stuff

No privacy

Clutter, clutter and clutter

8

Banish room gloom

Sad lampshades and ceiling lights

Drab, boring walls

Nowhere to display special things?

Can't find anything?

Boring furniture and none of it matches

HANDY MANDY

Hi, I'm Handy Mandy and I'm here to give advice, extra help and some great design idea opportunities that Clive and Jane may have forgotten to mention.
Here's my first piece of advice – rest easy, the projects in this book have been carefully chosen so that specialist tools and skills are not needed.

Banish room gloom

Treasure hunting

Look at all the bits and pieces around your house, in the garden and in the garage. Everyone hoards things 'just in case they need them'. Problem is, by the time they realise a use for them, they've forgotten where they've put them!

To turn forgotten, discarded and broken items that are no longer fashionable into the useful, beautiful and amazing means having a stockpile of odds and ends. Here are just a few of the many handy items worth hoarding –

- Fabric remnants are incredibly useful. Really sad bits of fabric can be used to protect furniture and floors when you're revamping, while others can be turned into wallhangings. Hoard pieces of felt because they can be cut into shapes to decorate a wallhanging.

- Old cotton bed sheets and duvets, the plainer the better, can be tie-dyed, used as a room divider or window and door blind.

- Curtains and curtain linings, and don't forget to keep the curtain hooks, rings and rod, as well.

- Find yourself a shoe box right now and label it 'Ribbons and Trimmings'. If you don't, you'll never be able to find these ever-so-useful bits when you need them. Look out for ribbons, lace, braid, string, cord, twine and any of the fancy ribbons and ties used in gift wrapping.

Banish room gloom

- Offcuts of hardboard, MDF, dowelling and any lengths of soft wood. (See page 23.)

- Lidded jars, plastic containers, bottles and food tins.

- Cork tiles are great because they can be used to make a pinboard among other things. Offcuts can be cut with a Stanley knife to make stencils and templates.

- Tins of almost-finished paint, especially the colour used to paint your room.

- Beads, sequins and fake gems can find their way into more revamping ideas than you've had hot dinners.

- Almost-empty spools of sewing or embroidery thread and left-over knitting wool.

This list could go on and on and on. When you start revamping you'll see potential in stuff that would otherwise have found its way into the bin.

Handy Mandy

Stockpiling materials for future use is great, but you have to store it so that it is not in the way and that it is easy for you to access. Simply stuffing it under your bed or on top of existing piles of 'treasure', won't work. Turn to pages 78, 113 and 115 for storage solutions.

Banish room gloom

Where to hunt

Apart from looking on all your family's discarded kit and household rubbish in a new light, there are other places to hunt for ideal makeover materials. Junk shops are quite rare in towns, despite what the TV designers say and the ones that do exist sometimes charge antique shop prices.

You're far more likely to have charity shops and bargain stores in your shopping centre. Some of these bargain stores sell everything for a pound and they stock all sorts of useful things. Before you turn your nose up and say, "They sell really naff things", remember what your task is – to turn naff into cool!

Banish room gloom

Other places to check out on a regular basis are car boot sales; bring and buy sales; swap and for sale ads in the local newspaper; the sale, discontinued and remnant tables in many shops you go into.

When is a chair, not a chair?

Sometimes we walk straight past an object because we don't really look at it. A broken chair, for example, may be well beyond repairing, but could you use the wood for another purpose? Could you turn that chair with the broken back into a stool, table or piece of sculpture? From now on, look beyond the obvious use of an object and look to what it is made off, what bits you could salvage for another purpose and ask yourself if there is something you can do with it.

A cracking idea

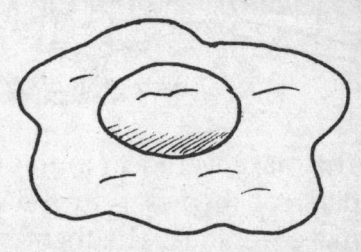

This small fried egg cushion is proof that something egg-tremely cool can be made without shelling out a penny or cent. All that was used was an old white sheet, some leftover yellow fabric and the stuffing from an old pillow and seat cushion.

Fold the white fabric in half, draw the fried egg shape and pin along the outline. Cut it out and then sew the two pieces together, leaving a 15 cm (6 in) opening. Turn inside out (to hide the stitching) and fill with stuffing. Close up the opening. Repeat to make the yolk. Place the yolk on the egg white and stitch in place.

Banish room gloom

Theme dream

The makeover ideas in this book have been divided between different themes. A theme is the 'subject' that links each makeover idea. The themes we've chosen are – fabulous fabric (Chapter 3), sport (Chapter 4), computers (Chapter 5), the great outdoors (Chapter 6), ghouls and creepy-crawlies (Chapter 7), and super sleuth (Chapter 8).

Within each chapter you'll find loads of ideas, but you must remember that all the ideas can be adapted to suit your chosen revamping theme. To pick and mix ideas, you may only have to choose a different colour or material, a different shape or different decoration. Don't forget to browse every chapter for ideas no matter which theme you've chosen.

Banish room gloom

Handy Mandy

Other theme ideas you might like to consider – tropical island, outer space, medieval, ultra-modern, Arabian nights, Inca Indian, transport, music, glitz and glam, seaside, romance, dance or hippy flower power.

Choosing and following-through on a theme will give your room a coordinated look, and when you start linking a number of different revamp ideas together, you are in real room makeover territory. A coordinated look is helped if you restrict the number of colours you use.

The makeover ideas in this book are just the start. Use your imagination to create your own designs. As far as we're concerned, the first and only rule of interior design for your room is – choose what you want in your room allowing for what you can make, the materials you have and what a parent will allow.

Old hat

Your tastes are likely to be fast-changing. Everyone goes through phases and what interested you two, three or more years ago may not be what you are interested in now. Knowing what will be taking your fancy in the future is a job for a fortune teller. That's why the majority of the ideas in this book are stand-alone. They'll work well in your room, but they're constructed in a way to make change easy.

Fools rush in

Don't rush off and start a project without knowing precisely what you're doing first. I know what I'm like – I get all excited, pile in without thinking an idea through – and end up in a right mess. Try to avoid being like me – it will pay off!

2 Let's get started

By now you're raring to get going on your room makeover, but please take a little time to first read about the nuts and bolts of the tools you may need, tips and techniques, and the sort of materials you'll be using. Keep referring to this chapter when you start on an idea – there's bound to be a tip or two that will save you time, energy and grief.

Somewhere to work

The ideal working area, especially for bigger jobs, is a sturdy bench or table in a shed or garage. Second-best is a table on a firm surface in the garden or on a verandah. (Good ventilation is crucial when painting or varnishing, for example.) If you're restricted to a corner inside your home, then the portable, fold-up work surface on page 108 could be just what you need.

No matter where you work, you should protect the work surface, nearby furniture and the surrounding floor with newspaper or painting and dust sheets. For hammering and cutting jobs, use a craft mat or a piece of smooth wood on top of the newspaper.

Let's get started

What to wear

Old clothes that cover your legs and arms, but make sure that the sleeves don't flap about and get in the way. Long hair should be tied back off your face. When painting, varnishing or sanding, wear a cap to help keep your hair clean. Also in your working clobber kit, you should have a pair of gloves (rubber or garden-type), a pair of goggles and a face mask. Goggles and face masks are very inexpensive, and should be worn when using certain types of paints or when drilling or sanding.

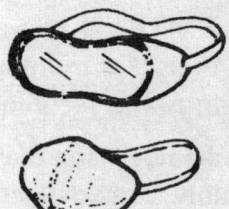
Goggles and face mask

Handy Mandy

There are some jobs that a parent won't let you attempt, and most of these involve power tools; any electric plugs, light fittings and switches; and saws. There is a good reason for their worry – these items can be hugely and seriously dangerous. Before starting a revamp idea, check it out with a parent and then agree on some limits – which bits you can do alone and which require adult help. Also agree on a place for you to work and what tools you can use. Break the agreement and your makeover days will be over.

For the ideas in this book, we have used the Aagrrh! system to show where adult help is recommended. Aagrrh! stands for Ask A Grown-Up, Responsible Reliable Housemate.

AAGRRH!

Let's get started

Tooling up

You will need access to, but not necessarily own, a number of tools. For more information about other types of tools, fittings and techniques, see the Glossary on pages 121-124.

Bradawl – sharp, pointy screwdriver-like tool that makes 'starter' holes for screws in softwoods and holes in card, cloth, leather and some plastics.

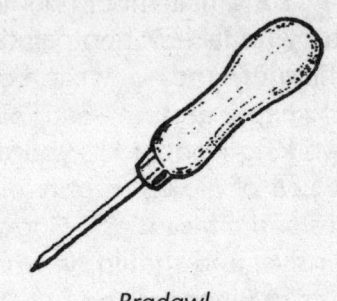
Bradawl

Craft knife – razor-sharp blade fixed in a handle and used for cutting paper and thin card. (See page 20.)

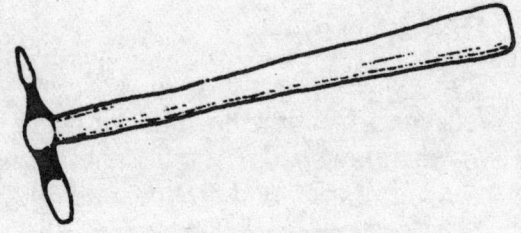
Panel-pin hammer

Hammer – a lightweight panel-pin hammer is best, though an adult may have to wield a heavier hammer to secure wall fittings.

Hand drill – turn the handle and the gears rotate so that a drill bit can make a hole in wood.

Hole punch – works like the hole punch you use for paper, but it cuts one hole at a time and the pressure on the cutting edge is supplied by being struck with a hammer.

Paintbrushes – you'll need small modelling and craft brushes, as well as 25 mm (1 in) and 50 mm (2 in) paintbrushes.

Let's get started

Pliers – great for holding things (see page 21), while the cutting edges can be used for cutting and stripping wire. Snub-nosed combi-pliers do two jobs. The strong, grooved plates are great for gripping and holding things (see page 21), while the blades can be used to cut and strip wire. You'll find the cutting edges just next to the gripping plates. If working on something small and fiddly, long-nosed pliers may be more suitable.

Snub-nosed combi pliers

Saws – you stick to using a small coping saw, and let an adult deal with an electric jigsaw or circular saw.

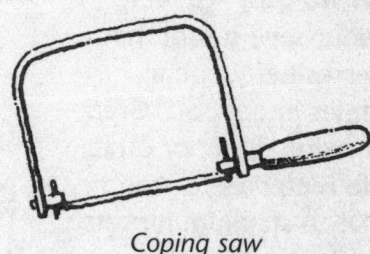

Coping saw

Scissors – ideally you should have two pairs – one for cutting paper and card, and another for cutting fabric. You may also need a pair of small scissors for cutting fiddly things.

Screwdriver – used to fit screws, so you will need access to a small and medium-sized straight-head screwdriver. You may also need a Philips-head screwdriver to fit screws with a crossed slot on the head.

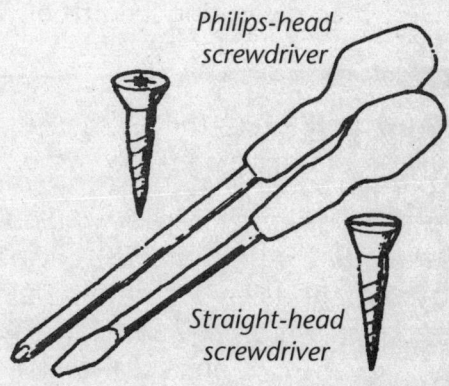

Philips-head screwdriver

Straight-head screwdriver

Let's get started

Stanley knife – razor-sharp knife suitable for cutting thick or corrugated card and cork tiles. When not in use, prevent accidents by pressing the blade of a Stanley knife or craft knife into a block of cork or wine bottle cork. Never leave dangerous tools like these on the floor or within reach of small children.

Stanley knife   *Craft knife*

Staple gun – a real labour-saving tool that presses hefty, metal staples into wood. Great for fixing fabric or other thin materials to wood or MDF. A staple gun costs a little less than the price of a double CD.

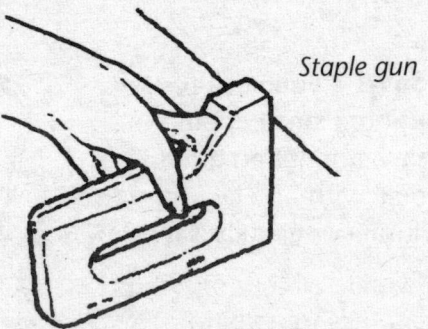

Staple gun

Steel rule – vital bit of kit if cutting a straight line using a craft or Stanley knife.

Tape measure – easier to use than your plastic school ruler when measuring lengths of wood or your room.

Handy Mandy

Your tool kit should also contain a black lead pencil, an eraser, a notebook for jotting down measurements and designs, a length of dowel for stirring paint, fine and medium grade sandpaper and cloths for wiping spills and your hands.

Let's get started

Tool tips

Bradawl

This is how you use a bradawl to make a starter hole for a screw in softwoods.

Press down and turn the handle in one direction to make the hole. Remove bradawl by turning in the opposite direction

Hold bradawl upright. If it tilts, the hole will be crooked

A cross marks the spot for the starter hole

Handy things, pliers

If you're all thumbs when it comes to holding, positioning or cutting something small and fiddly, use pliers to hold the item.

Use pliers when cutting thick card or a sharp-edged material with scissors

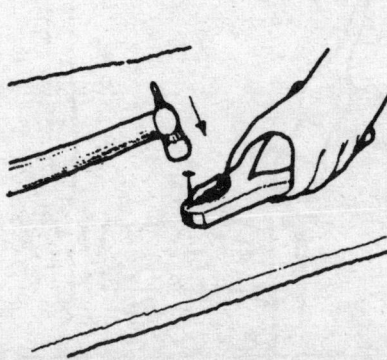

It's easier to screw a cup hook into wood or MDF, if you grip the hook with pliers

Save your fingers and let pliers steady a nail when it is being hammered

Let's get started

Cutting edge `AAGRRH!`

Follow this technique to make straight cuts using a steel rule and craft or Stanley knife. When cutting curved lines, follow the same safety code – **KEEP YOUR FINGERS AWAY FROM THE BLADE and WATCH WHAT YOU'RE DOING!**

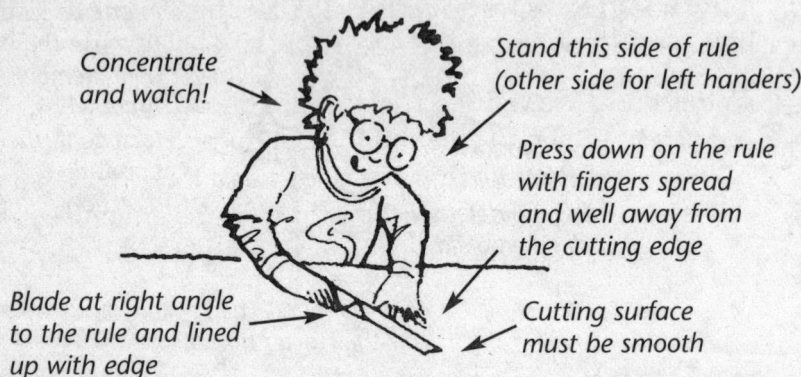

Concentrate and watch!

Stand this side of rule (other side for left handers)

Press down on the rule with fingers spread and well away from the cutting edge

Blade at right angle to the rule and lined up with edge

Cutting surface must be smooth

Move the blade smoothly and slowly down the item, but NEVER remotely close to you. If something is really long, do it in stages – move the material up and the ruler down the line you are cutting.

Hammering the point home

Always measure the length of the nail alongside the pieces of wood to be joined. The nail must be a little shorter than the combined depth. (This also applies to screws.) Make a small introductory hole with just the tip of a bradawl and then push the nail with your thumb into the 'dip'. Never take wild swings with a hammer – always use short, firm taps.

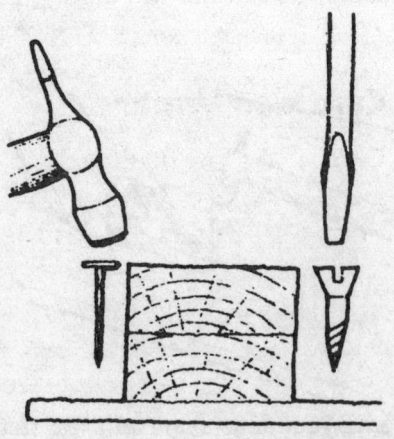

Let's get started

Raw materials

Wood

Most of the wood you're likely to lay your hands on is either hardboard or MDF, or light yellow-coloured softwoods like pine. Softwoods, unlike hardwoods, are easier to saw and join, are cheaper and can be drilled easily with a hand drill.

In this book, we've used sheets of hardboard and MDF, lengths of softwood (25 mm by 25 mm or 25 mm by 50 mm) and dowelling. Dowelling is a round, wooden rod and comes in lots of widths. In some revamp ideas, pea sticks or bamboo garden canes can be used instead of dowelling.

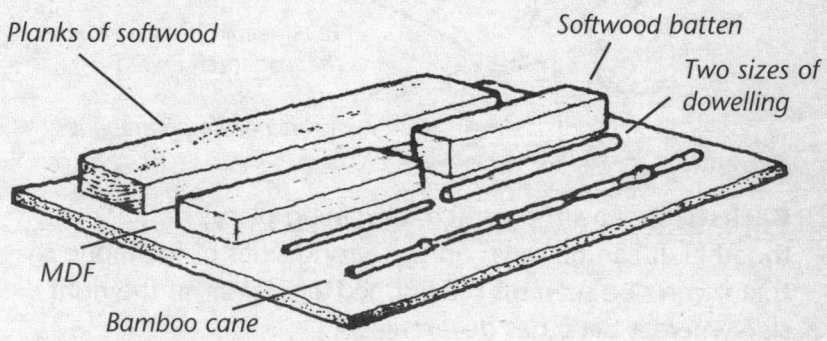

Planks of softwood
Softwood batten
Two sizes of dowelling
MDF
Bamboo cane

Card and paper

Card – you will need scrap pieces of thin and thick card, as well as sheets of card.
Corrugated card – this is the material used to make cardboard boxes. It consists of a layer of 'wavy' card sandwiched between layers of heavy paper.
Sugarpaper – a heavy paper, which comes in lots of colours can be bought in sheets or rolls from craft shops or stationers.
Paper – keep a good supply of coloured and recycled paper, giftwrap and newspaper to hand.

Let's get started

Fabric

Fabric is a top makeover material that can be stitched, glued, stapled and even nailed into position. On page 29, there's a list of fabrics that you might want to use.

You sew and sew!

The two types of stitch you are most likely to use in projects is the backstitch and the blanket stitch. Always use a double thickness of thread, knotted at the end, and a largish needle.

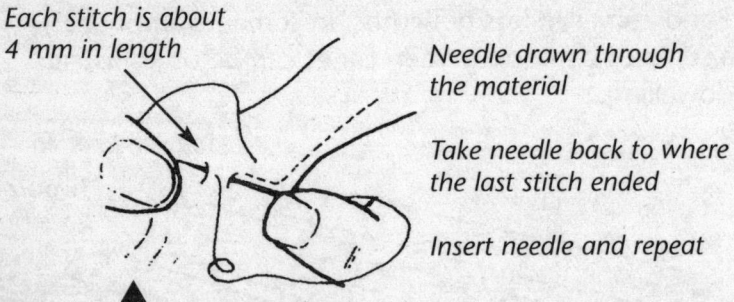

Each stitch is about 4 mm in length

Needle drawn through the material

Take needle back to where the last stitch ended

Insert needle and repeat

▲

Backstitch – a strong stitch for joining pieces of fabric together. It can be sewn on the wrong sides of the fabric so that it can't be seen on the finished article, or on the right side where it becomes decorative.

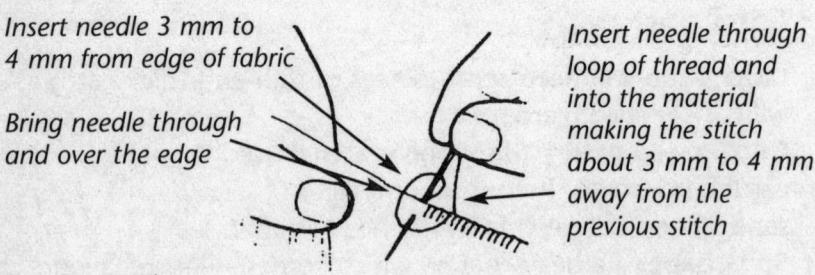

Insert needle 3 mm to 4 mm from edge of fabric

Bring needle through and over the edge

Insert needle through loop of thread and into the material making the stitch about 3 mm to 4 mm away from the previous stitch

▲

Blanket stitch – a chain of stitches that is sewn as a decorative edging to join fabrics together or to hem.

Glue news

Compared to any other way of fixing two bits of stuff together, glue is the business. It's quick, easy and, providing you prepare the surfaces and use the right type of glue, it makes a strong bond. A prepared surface is clean and dry, and dust- and grease-free.

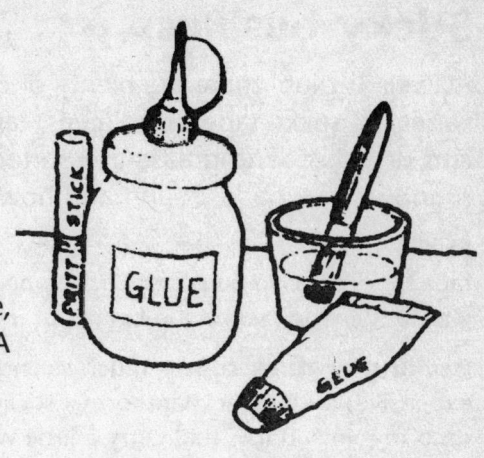

After use, wipe around the cap to remove excess glue and then reseal tightly.

One of the most useful, all-round glues is a white craft glue (sometimes called PVA glue). This glue can be used on paper, fabric, wood and some plastics, and it dries to a clear finish. A little of this glue goes a long way, so spread it evenly and wipe away excess. Many companies make a glue and label it 'craft glue'. Before buying read the label – it should say solvent-free and water-based. For a stronger bond between pieces of wood, use a wood glue and follow the instructions on the container.

When gluing paper to paper, you can use a stick of paper glue. The only other paste you will need is wallpaper paste.

Always apply a glue thinly and evenly all over the surfaces using a piece of stiff card as a spreader.

Let's get started

Sticky business

As well as glue, there are plenty of opportunities to use a variety of sticky tapes. Like glues, tapes work best on clean and dry, dust- and grease-free surfaces. Here's a quick rundown of what's around and how to use it –

Sticky tape – use clear tape for almost-invisible joins and coloured tape for decorative purposes. Sticky tape is great for paper-to-paper jobs, but it won't withstand being put under stress.

Packing or duck tape – much stronger (therefore more expensive) and wider than normal sticky tape, these tapes can be used to join surfaces that carry a little weight. They do not come in deadly attractive colours and can't be painted over, so use on hidden joins only.

Double-sided tape – this looks like normal tape, except that both sides are sticky. Cut off the length of tape you need, press the exposed sticky side onto one surface, peel off the protective layer from the other side and press it firmly onto the surface to be joined.

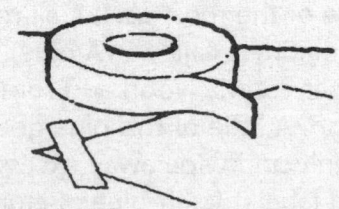

Make sure that your fingers and the surfaces to be taped are clean and dry before cutting and positioning any type of adhesive tape.

Double-sided, self-adhesive pads – both sides of these spongy pads or strips are very sticky. If used correctly and in sufficient numbers they can secure medium-weight objects onto a wall.

Sticky tack – this Plasticine-like material can be moulded and used to stick posters and other paper items onto walls. It is easily removed.

Masking tape – used to cover areas that you don't want painted. Long strips of masking tape let you paint straight stripes easily. You can also buy masking tape that bends to create curved lines.

Let's get started

Paint magic

A new coat of paint can transform the saddest item. In this book, we suggest using household paints because their finish is water-resistant and long-lasting and the colour range vast. This does not mean that watercolour or acrylic paints can't be used. (See page 106.) Emulsion, gloss and varnish, and metal and spray paints are designed to be used for different purposes, and you can find out about them in the Glossary on pages 121-124.

Painting tips

1. Protect nearby surfaces and the floor and wear old clothes.
2. Paint outdoors or in a room with doors and windows opened.
3. Any surface to be painted should be cleaned thoroughly.
4. Different paints work in different ways, so always read and follow the instructions on the pot or tin.
5. Use a small brush for small areas; a larger brush for bigger areas.
6. Dip the brush into the paint, gently wipe both sides against the inside edge of the tin and paint using up-and-down or side-to-side strokes.
7. If a blob of paint runs, quickly use the brush to even it out.
8. Use a stick to stir the paint so that the colour is even.
9. If you stop painting for a short time, wrap the brush in plastic film. When you finish painting for the day, wash the brush following the instructions on the paint tin. Some paints can be washed out with water; others need brush cleaner or white spirit. (Check with an adult first.) Rub the clean brush on newspaper before storing it handle down.
10. Reseal the paint pot or tin tightly.

 It's a material world

There are seven absolutely and utterly compelling reasons for using fabric somewhere in your decorating scheme.

1 It is easy to cut.
2 It can be secured using sewing needle and thread, glue, stationery staples or a staple gun.
3 You can buy remnants cheaply, or ask permission to raid the 'too-good-to-throw-away' box of old bedding and curtains, and left-over fabrics and trimmings.
4 Fabric can be used almost anywhere and over most surfaces.
5 You can find fabrics and patterns to suit all colour schemes and decorating themes. Fabric really is your flexible best friend.
6 They add texture.
7 Great looks can be achieved really quickly!

Are you compelled? Are you ready to cut the cotton, fold the fake fur and vamp with velvet!

Touchy, feely

Different fabrics have different textures. The texture determines how it feels when you rub it against your skin, what it looks like and what it can be used for. Here are some fabrics that could find their way into your room –

  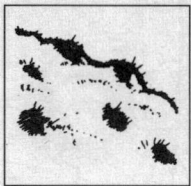 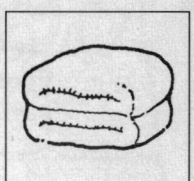

Satin and velvet – smooth with a shiny finish.

Vinyl – shiny, cold, dead-smooth and plastic-like with a fabric backing.

Fake fur and fleece – downright cuddly fabrics.

Blanket fabric, felt, wool and towelling – soft yet hard-wearing.

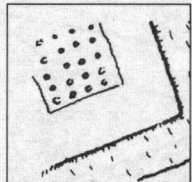 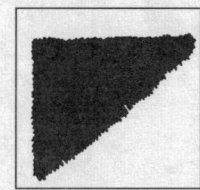 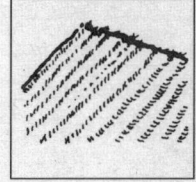

Cotton and calico – flat and smooth, or woven to give a knobbly texture.

Hessian (sacking) – coarse, rough and brown in colour. It frays easily.

Corduroy – soft and sort of cuddly with raised ridges.

Where to find

If your rummage through the 'too-good-to-throw-away' pile is unsuccessful, try the remnant box in fabric shops or car boot sales, charity shops, and bring-and-buy sales. Don't just look out for remnant fabrics, but also for curtains and linings, sheets and pillow cases, duvet covers, towels, rugs and throws and even clothes. A pre-loved winter wool coat, for example, can be cut to make a seat or cushion cover. Remember, it's the fabric you want, not the item. Once in your talented hands, tat becomes treasure!

It's a material world

What you can do

This room is full of fabric inspiration, and you'll find the how-to instructions on pages 32-41.

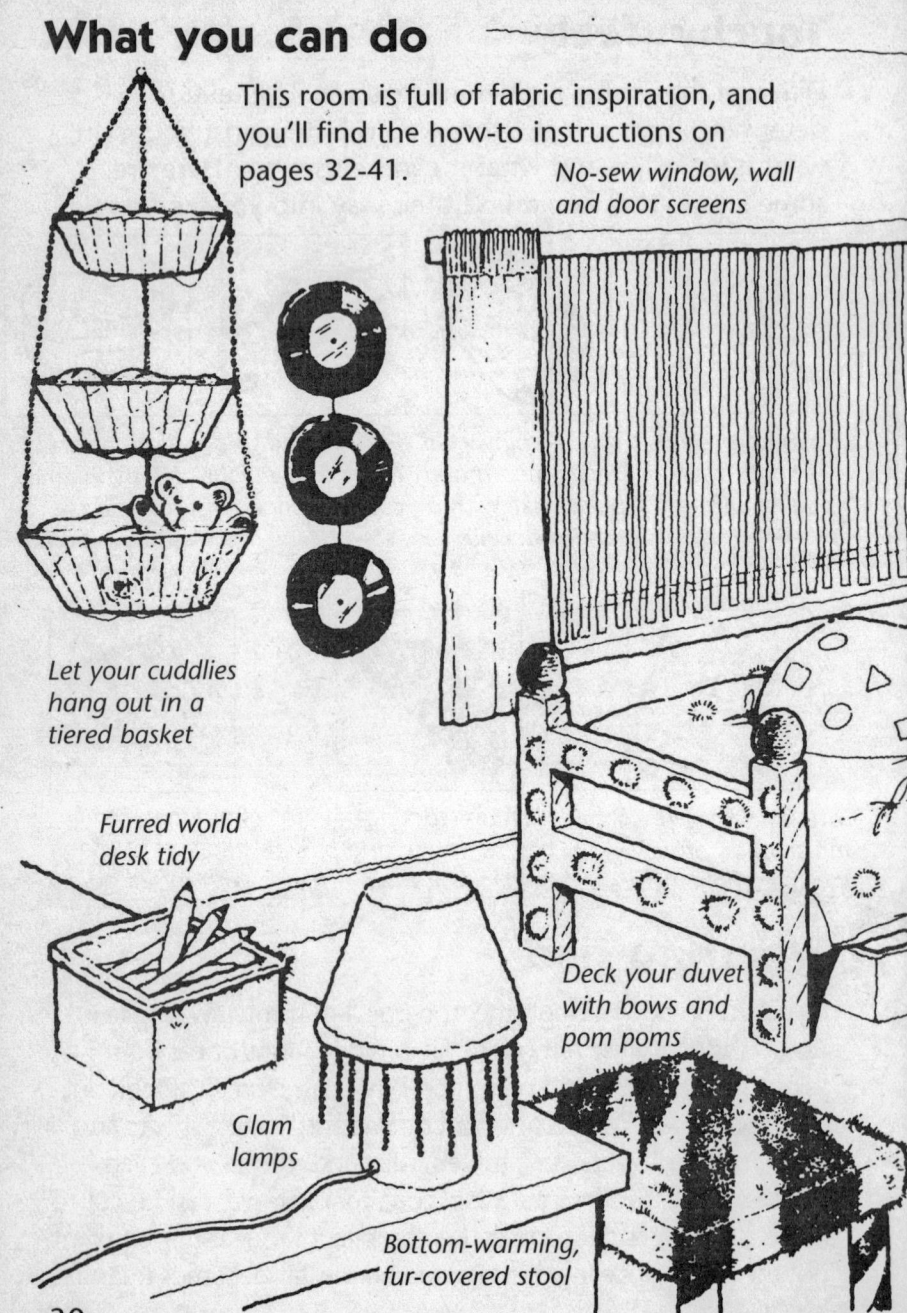

No-sew window, wall and door screens

Let your cuddlies hang out in a tiered basket

Furred world desk tidy

Deck your duvet with bows and pom poms

Glam lamps

Bottom-warming, fur-covered stool

It's a material world

Light up your life

Is the crowning glory of your bedside or ceiling lamp as boring as a double maths lesson? Yes, then here are three ways to make the switch from ghastly to glam.

Half 'n' half

STEP 1 AAGRRH!

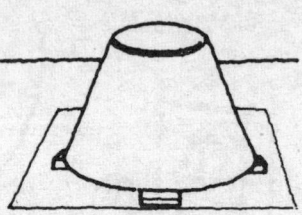

Ask an adult to remove the shade from the lamp base or ceiling fixture. Rest the shade on three small pieces of wood over a large sheet of paper. Brush the shade to remove dust.

STEP 2

Using a pencil and ruler, divide the shade into two (or more, if you like) equal segments. Paint each segment a different colour using matt emulsion paint. Allow to dry between coats and before decorating.

This shade is divided into four segments

Buttons, beads and baubles

You can decorate your lampshade with flat buttons and fake gems, ribbons, feathers, sequins, shells, pom-poms and even wobbly goo-goo eyes. These can be attached to the shade with white craft glue or double-sided tape. Go one step further and use sewing needle and thread to attach beads around the lower edge.

It's a material world

Knot the thread and push the needle through the first (the lowest hanging) bead two times, then thread on the remaining beads. Push the needle through the shade towards the inside, remove the needle and tie the thread.

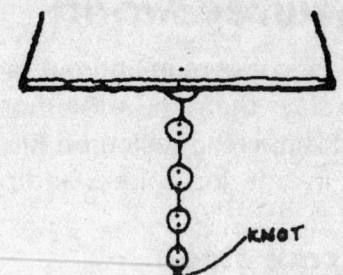

Going the hole way

Instead of sticking stuff onto the shade, you can play light games by peppering a sad, old plain shade with small holes or slits. You can make the holes using a hole punch and small hammer, or with a Stanley knife and metal rule.

Lay the shade on its side and resting on a block of wood. Position the hole punch and hold it steady while giving it a firm tap with a hammer. Spread the holes evenly or draw, in pencil, a pattern to follow.

Make two straight or wavy slits in the shade very close together, then cut across the top and bottom to remove the thin sliver of shade fabric. Always do the cutting on a piece of wood and keep fingers well out of the way. AAGRRH!

It's a material world

The furred world

Furry fabric moves in and out of fashion, but one thing always stays the same – the more radical the fur, the better it looks. Plain, cream-coloured fur gets about 4 out of 10; furry fabrics in amazing colours and patterns scores full marks.

One cool stool

No one will guess that the hot but cool fur conceals the original padded, plastic seat of an old kitchen stool. We've used cow-styled fur here. If that doesn't suit your moo...d, try a different pattern.

STEP 1 ▶
Lay the stool upside-down on a piece of paper or newspaper that is larger than the seat. Trace the outline of the seat onto the paper.

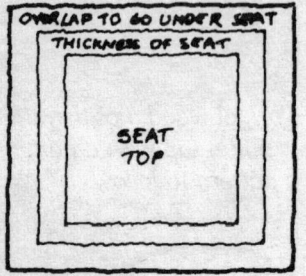

◀ **STEP 2**
Measure the thickness of the seat and add this to your newspaper pattern. Then, add another 5 cm (2 in) for overlap to the base of the seat. Cut out your pattern.

STEP 3 ▶
Pin the pattern to the wrong side of the fur and cut around it. Remove the pins and place the fabric wrong side up on your work surface.

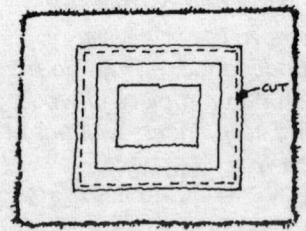

It's a material world

STEP 4 ▶

Place the stool onto the centre of the fabric, and cut into the fabric (as shown) to make covering the corners easier. Apply glue evenly to the base of the seat, then bring the fabric over the edge and press down firmly. For extra hold, use a staple gun to secure the fabric to the base of the seat.

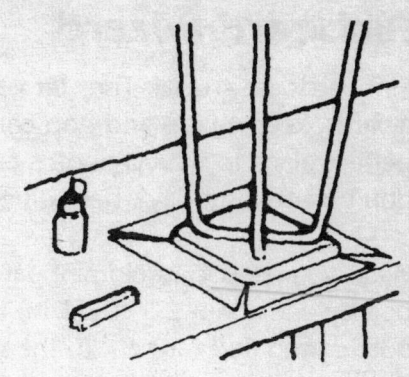

You have upholstered your first piece of furniture. Congratulations! Drawing and cutting out a paper pattern is the key, and can be applied to almost any cover-up job.

More furry ideas

Mirror and picture frames, plastic and corrugated cardboard storage boxes and desk tidies, and stereo speaker boxes are perfect for a furry makeover. A thin strip of fur can be used as a trim along the edge of a desk.

Because there are few stresses on the fabric, it can be attached to picture frames, storage boxes and the rest with white craft glue or with double-sided tape. Ask for permission before furring up any pieces of furniture.

Pinboard wizard

Pinboards are crucial. They let you show off your certificates and awards, keep invites and pop concert tickets safe, and are the perfect place to pin up photos of 'this week's' fave idol – you don't want yesterday's hero glued to your wall forever, do you?

What you need is an old pinboard, a biggish sheet of polystyrene about 2.5 cm (1 in) thick or three pieces of heavy-duty corrugated card cut to the same size and glued together. You can buy polystyrene in craft shops and some DIY sheds, or you can recycle the polystyrene that is used as protective packing for computers, TVs and large appliances. These boxes will also yield sturdy corrugated card. In addition, you'll need a piece of fabric that will cover the front and sides (plus overlap onto the back) of your pinboard, white craft glue and lots of 15 mm ($^1/_2$ in) wide ribbon or bias binding (you can buy this inexpensively in fabric shops). The ribbons or bias binding can be in one colour, footie team colours or a rainbow of colours.

STEP 1
Lay the fabric wrong side up on your work surface, smooth any bumps or wrinkles and then place your 'pinboard' in the centre. Cut the corners, as shown, to make the finish neater.

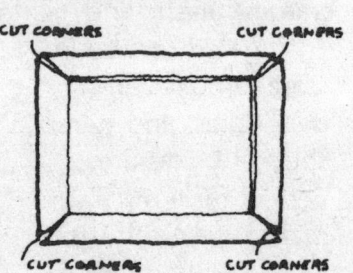

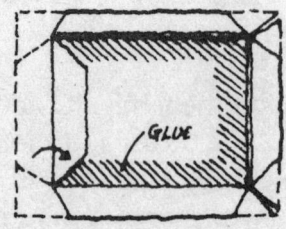

◀ STEP 2
Apply glue to the sides and around the edge of the 'pinboard'. Fold the fabric over the edges and press it firmly into the glue. Allow the glue to dry.

STEP 3 ▶

Turn the pinboard over and position ribbons, as shown. Leave 15 cm (6 in) between each ribbon and make sure the ribbons are long enough to be secured to the back of the board. Keep the ribbons in place with sticky tape or drawing pins.

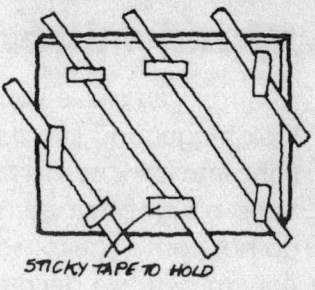
STICKY TAPE TO HOLD

◀ **STEP 4**

Turn the pinboard over and glue, then staple gun, the ribbons to the side and back of the pinboard, making sure the ribbons are pulled taut. If the ribbons are loose, your bits and pieces will slip off the pinboard. When the glue is dry, remove the sticky tape or drawing pins.

STEP 5 ▶

Weave lengths of ribbon under and over the attached ribbons, making sure the ribbon is long enough to overlap onto the back of the pinboard. Use the same spacing as before, and hold the ribbons in place with tape or drawing pins. Repeat step 4 to secure the ribbons.

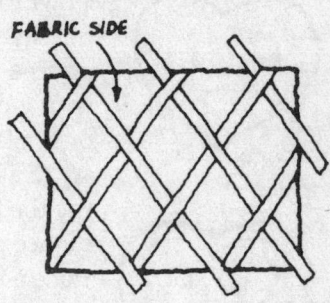
FABRIC SIDE

When dry, slip papers between the ribbons and the board. You can lean the board against a wall or mount it onto a wall using cord or rope threaded through holes made in the top two corners of the pinboard. Hang the cord from a hook.

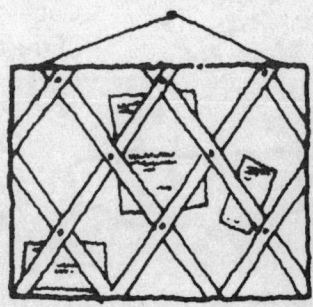

It's a material world

Mirror, mirror on the wall

A mirror can make your room look bigger and can reflect light into dark corners. Shop-bought framed mirrors do not come cheap, so here's how to perform decorating magic with a mirror.

Heart to heart

You will need – a sheet of polystyrene or three sheets of corrugated card glued together, Stanley knife, felt-tip pen, a piece of furry fabric, a small mirror, craft glue and a length of cord.

◀ STEP 1
Draw the heart-shaped outline onto the polystyrene or corrugated card. Cut it out using a Stanley knife. (Don't forget to protect your working surface with a sheet of hardboard or similar.)

◀ STEP 2
Lay the fur fabric, wrong side up, on your work surface and place the heart-shape in the centre. Trace around it with a felt-tip pen. Then draw a second outline 5 cm (2 in) outside the tracing. Cut around this line. Lay the mirror in the centre of the fabric and trace around it. Cut out the tracing of the mirror.

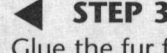

◀ STEP 3
Glue the fur fabric to the heart-shaped card. Turn the card over and snip into the fabric, as shown. Apply glue around the edge of the card and fold over the fabric. Apply pressure to the fabric to make sure it sticks firmly.

It's a material world

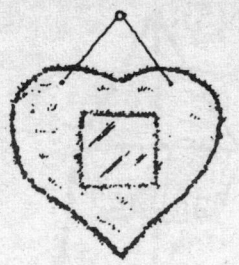

◀ STEP 4
Turn the frame over and glue the mirror onto the card, brushing the fur fabric out of the way. Make two holes in the top of the frame with a bradawl and thread through and firmly knot the cord.

Mirrors in a minute

Can't handle making a backing for a round mirror, then use an old vinyl record. A parent may have one that they no longer want, or you can pick them up (sometimes very cheaply) from a car boot sale or junk shop. Follow steps as above to make a furry frame, or simply glue non-furry fabric to the record and then firmly glue the mirror to the fabric.

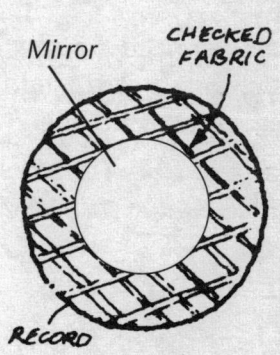

If you have a mirror with a boring frame, you can give it a new look using ribbon bows, felt cut-outs, glitter and sequins. Fix your decorations to the frame with craft glue.

Deco in a dash
Basket of cuddlies

Weave lengths of ribbon in and out of the metal frames of hanging baskets to make a cosy home for your favourite cuddlies. Hold the ends of the ribbons in place with a little tape stuck to the inside of the basket or with small safety pins. Suspend the basket from a ceiling hook or from the hanging rail inside a wardrobe.

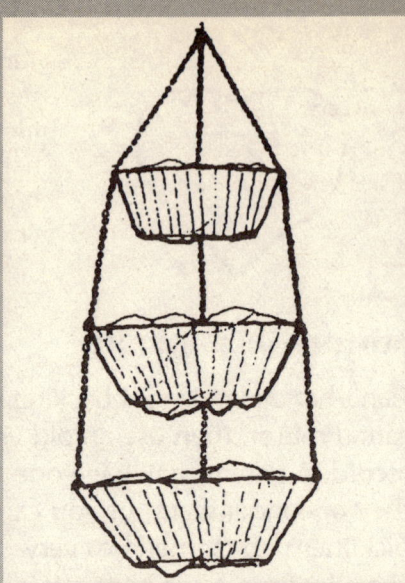

Bows and balls

Tie lots of ribbon bows and buy small pom-poms from a craft shop and then stitch them to the upper surface of your duvet cover. (Remove the duvet first.) You can also use bows, pom-poms and buttons to decorate cushion covers, fabric lamp-shades, curtains and even the cosy-toes floor rug that follows.

Cosy-toes rug

Decide on a shape for your floor rug, then cut out two pieces of blanket fabric the same size or one piece of fur fabric and one piece of blanket fabric (this is a backing for the fur fabric). Put the two pieces of fabric wrong-sides together, then blanket stitch (see page 24) neatly all around the edge to join the pieces together. So that your stitching shows up, thread a large-eyed sewing needle with thick cotton or embroidery thread or knitting wool. Stop the rug slipping on a wooden floor with double-sided tape or with special webbing you can buy in flooring or DIY stores.

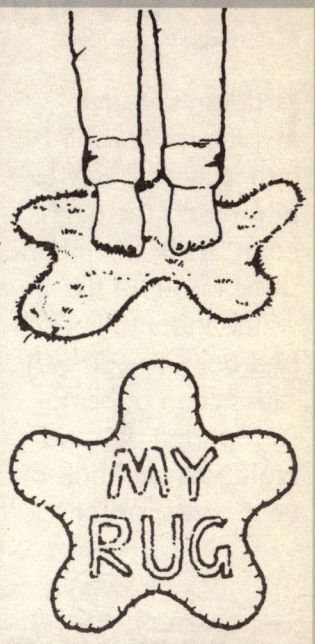

Screen stars

You can adapt this window dressing (that's the fancy name designers use for curtains) to make a screen for a door or a wall decoration. Ask an adult to cut a piece of dowelling to the length you need, then loop one end of a length (this will depend on how long you want the screen) of wide

ribbon or strip of fabric over the dowelling. Staple the ribbon together close to the dowelling. Repeat until the dowelling is covered. Rest your screen on existing curtain hooks or screw-in hooks.

 # Designs on sport

It doesn't matter which sport you're into, there's a way to bring it off the pitch, court, track, circuit and slope or out of the water and into your bedroom. Imagine the satisfaction of being surrounded day and night with symbols of your fave sport or sports.

There's isn't space to feature each idea for every sport, so use your loaf to apply an idea to your sport. Sometimes the switch is simply a matter of swapping a running shoe for a studded boot, or basketball strip for judo gear. In other instances, you may have to rough-out plans for your version of an idea.

Get it right

If you're not 100 per cent sure which symbols best represent a sport or exactly what they look like, then it's time for some research. All the best interior designers thoroughly research a decorating theme before they prise the lid off that first tin of paint.

Designs on sport

One thing you must get right is colour. Team colours are critical, so when looking for paint or fabric don't rely on your memory, take along the strip or jersey, a colour photo from a magazine or a banner or badge and compare it with the paint chip or fabric under natural light; fluorescent lighting does strange things to colour.

Chips, please

What's a paint chip? It's a sample of a paint colour that is applied to a piece of card and then dried. In the paint departments of hardware or DIY stores there are booklets and strips of paint chips piled high. Take a selection that comes close to the colours you're after, then check them out under natural light. There's no need to buy whopper tins of paint, you can buy small test pots of water-based paint and still have change from your pocket money. Gloss paint (see page 122) or hobby paint is usually available in small tins.

If you can't find the right colour in a fabric or want to recycle some fabric, then ask an adult to help you buy and use a cold-water dye. They are not expensive and the colours are true if the fabric is white or pale coloured. Always follow the instructions that come with the dye – the preparation, measurements and timings are fairly critical.

Handy Mandy

The easiest sort of household paint to use is emulsion. It is water-based so small drips can be quickly cleaned up with a damp cloth, and brushes can be cleaned in water and washing-up detergent. Emulsion dries quickly and you can make a little go a long way by adding a small amount of water.

Designs on sport

What you can do

This bedroom is full of sport-inspired decoration, and you'll find the how-to instructions on pages 46-55.

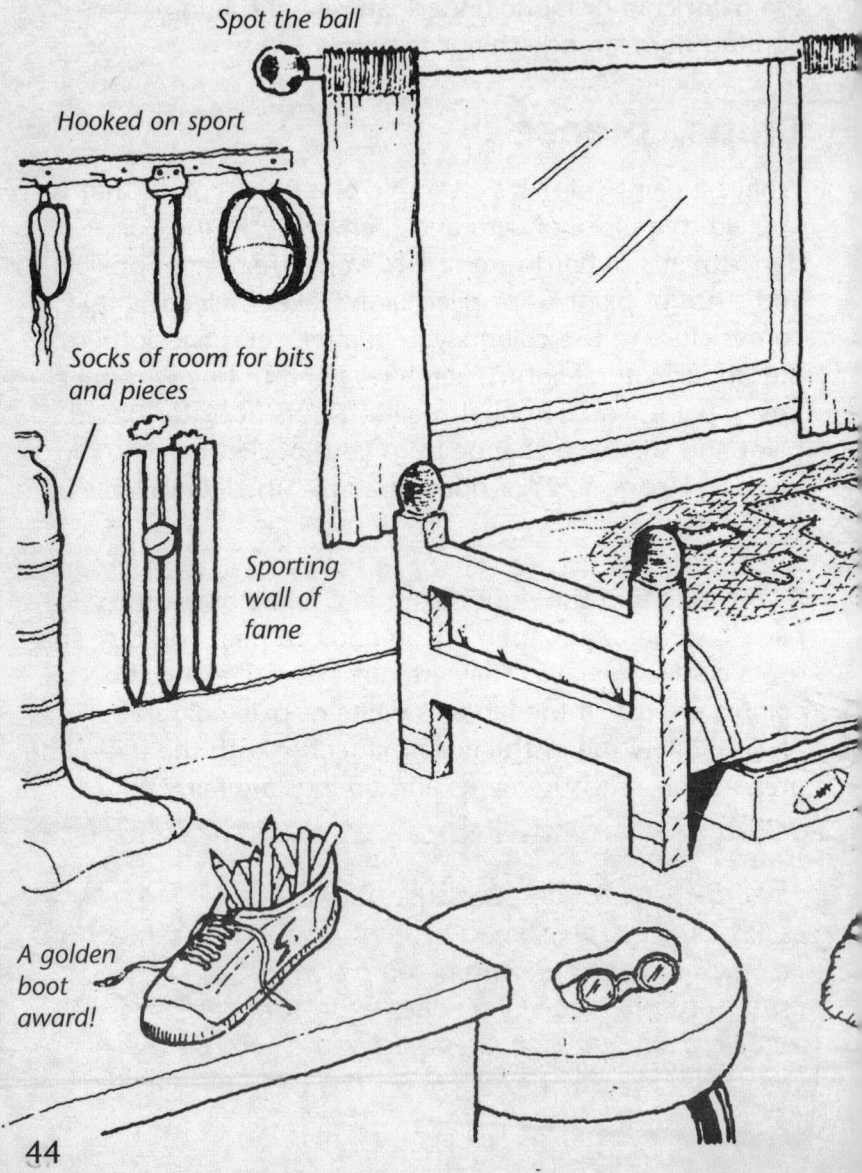

Spot the ball

Hooked on sport

Socks of room for bits and pieces

Sporting wall of fame

A golden boot award!

Designs on sport

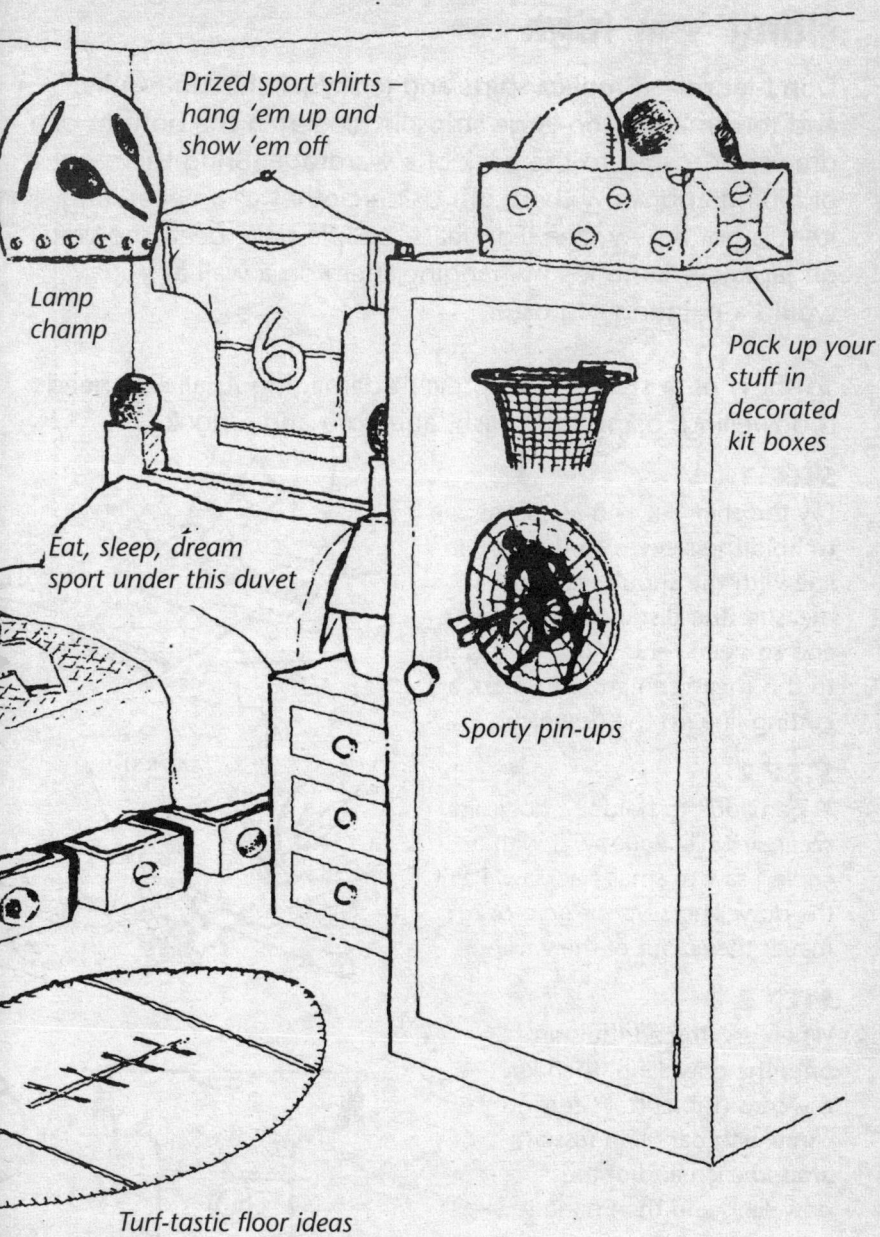

Designs on sport

Hang 'em high

Don't let prized replica shirts and jerseys, T-shirt souvenirs, and too-small or too-large strips lie hidden in the bottom of a drawer or tossed to the back of a wardrobe. Bring them out of hiding and show them off! Using clothes as a decorating item is not a new idea. For years, people have been showing off Japanese kimonos by hanging them on a wall as you would a painting or poster.

To show off a shirt and to prevent damaging it, all you need is dowelling, paint and brush, and cord and a hook.

STEP 1 ▶
Lay the shirt flat and ask someone to hold the sleeves so they are in line with the shoulders and measure the distance from sleeve end to sleeve end. Add 5 cm (2 in) to this measurement and mark a cutting line on the dowelling.

STEP 2 ▶
Ask an adult to hold the dowelling securely while you saw it with a coping saw or small hacksaw. Paint the dowelling silver or gold or to match the colour of the wall.

STEP 3 ▶
When dry, thread the shirt onto the dowelling, then knot the cord (this curtain cord came with dangling tassels) around each end of the dowelling and then hang it on a hook fixed into the wall.

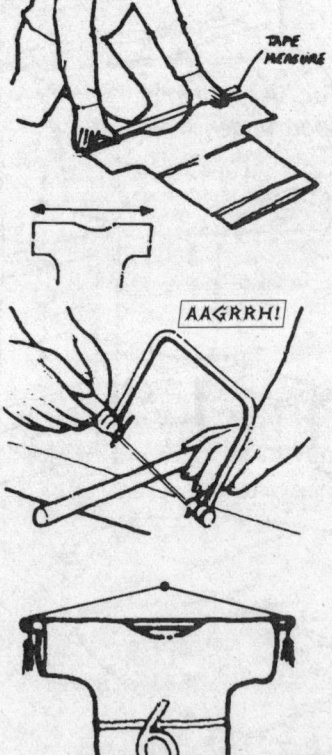

Designs on sport

Happy sporting dreams

If you've got a complete sports outfit that you know you'll never need again, then this unique duvet is for you. What you need is a plain duvet cover; old sports shirt, shorts and socks; scissors and sewing stuff. A sewing machine does the best job and does it quickly, but if that's impossible then it's time to thread a sewing needle and look for willing volunteers. Though a time-consuming job, the end result is so worth it!

STEP 1 ▶
Lay the shirt, shorts and socks out smoothly on a flat surface and cut along the side, sleeve and shoulder seams so that you get a front and back piece for each item. The 'fronts' will go on one side of the duvet, the 'backs' on the other.

STEP 2 ▶
Pin the 'front' pieces to the duvet, turning under a hem to neaten the cut edges. Leave a gap between the shorts and the socks. Use a backstitch (see page 24) to sew the pieces in place, making sure you only sew through one layer of duvet fabric. Repeat to sew the 'back' pieces to the other side of the duvet.

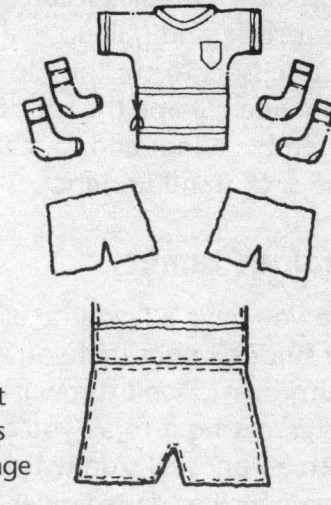

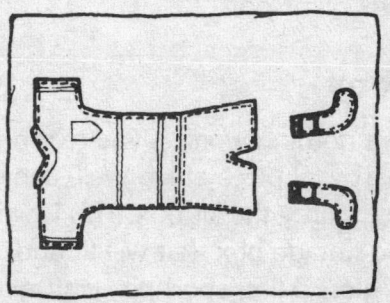

Sweet sporting dreams are made of this.

Hold alls

Sock it to 'em

Turn an old football or hockey sock into a handy (or footy!) container for bits and pieces. Fill the toe and halfway along the foot of the sock with small stones. Find a drinks bottle that will slip securely into your sock, and pull up the sock. Use scissors to cut the top off the container. Shape the sock to resemble a foot and to make the sock stand upright.

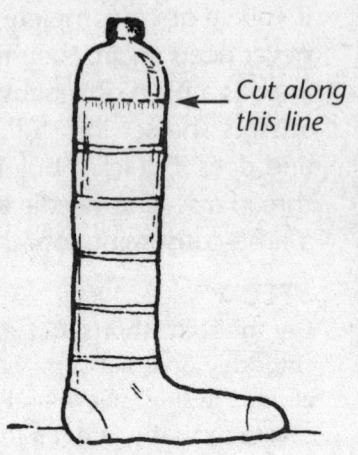

← Cut along this line

Trainer tamer

Do you have a favourite old trainer or studded boot that you've outgrown? Don't throw it away. After leaving it to air you can turn it into an unusual trophy that doubles as a pencil or darts holder. Clean the shoe, then paint it gold or silver. Use the shoe as it is, or wedge a plastic container into the foot hole to make a novel plant pot.

Kit box

There's nothing worse – you're running late and you can't find that last vital piece of kit. Well, panic no more because here is the solution – the kit box. This is what you need – a cheapy, plastic storage box that will fit under your bed or sit safely on a shelf, gloss paint, sport pix, craft glue, and clear matt varnish.

Designs on sport

Lay the storage box on layers of paper, decide on a pattern and then gloss paint the outside of the box. (It may take two coats.) Then, use the glue to stick on the pictures. When dry, apply a coat of clear matt varnish over the pictures to protect them.

These kit boxes have been painted then decorated with tennis, swimming, golf and equestrian images.

You're hooked

If it's small bits of kit that are the problem, then it's hooks, clamps and hinged clips that you need. Fixing hooks into the edge of a wooden shelf or inside a wardrobe is simply a matter of screwing them in, while clamps and clips can be secured with a screw or nail. If you can't use an existing wooden surface, then get your mitts on a length of wood or a piece of MDF. Attach your hooks, clamps and clips, then ask an adult to fix the wood or MDF to a wall. AAGRRH!

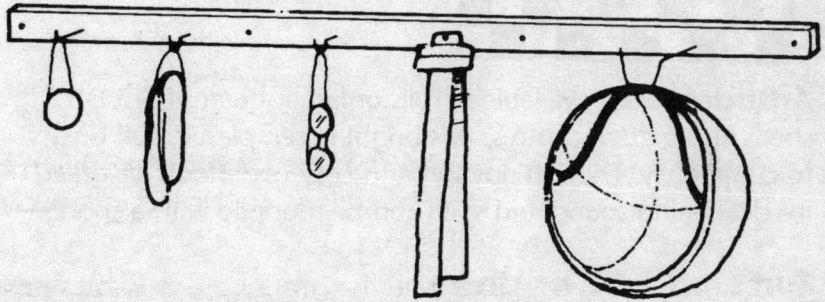

If well-secured (this wooden strip is fixed to a wall with four hefty screws), large hooks, clips and clamps can be used for big bits of kit.

Designs on sport

Try this pitch

Would you like the floor in your bedroom to look like a football pitch, cricket crease, golf or bowling green, or lawn tennis court? Yes! I hear you scream. It's dead simple and has nothing to do with tearing up the garden. All you need are green carpet squares or better still, artificial turf.

Carpet squares – these can be bought in packs and they come in lots of colours. This means that you can design a pattern that best reflects your sport. There is also scope with carpet tiles to cut them (adult help a must) to create court markings.

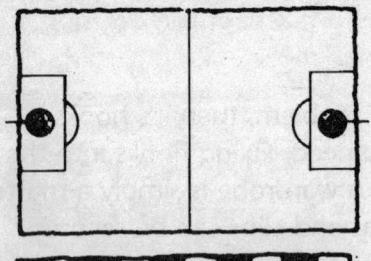

This simplified pitch design involves lots of cutting as each marking is made from narrow strips of carpet square.

Vroom! The chequered flag look for someone who's into motor racing.

Artificial turf – available in rolls or large squares from DIY sheds and garden centres, this bright green plastic stuff is easy to cut and lay. Though not soft and cosy underfoot, it's great for deadening sound and spills can be mopped with a sponge.

Turf's up . . . or down

There's perhaps only one problem – convincing the adults in your life that wall-to-wall turf is the business. To help you convince them, here's the low-down –

Designs on sport

1. The existing flooring stays where it is; the new covering is laid on top.
2. Existing flooring will last longer because it will be protected from abuse by muddy trainers and running spikes.
3. Carpet squares and artificial turf are low maintenance and super hard-wearing.
4. Easy to remove because there's no glue or tape involved.
5. You'll forgo all pocket money and treats to pay for the stuff, and you'll do extra chores in order to prove just how much you need to turf you room.

If they are not convinced and say no, accept the decision. Don't push it too hard, or you may receive a red card.

Handy Mandy

Both carpet tiles and artificial turf can be painted, though the finish will not be perfect and may wear off quickly. To make a good job of say marking court lines, first do a design on paper and then 'outline' the areas of flooring to be painted with masking tape. Don't try to do anything complicated, keep your design dead simple.

Paint applied gently with a smallish brush or small roller to avoid spatters

Masking tape either side of the area to be painted

Cover nearby furniture and surfaces and rest a small container of paint on sheets of newspaper. Allow the paint to dry before removing the masking tape.

Designs on sport

Sporting walls of fame

Posters of your favourite sport or sporting heroes have their place, but for something special how about creating your own piece of sporting art-cum-sculpture? Sounds complicated, but it isn't and the basic idea can be applied to lots of sports. The following life-size homage to cricket shows three stumps, ball and flying bails, and is glued to the wall at floor level. Because art-cum-sculpture is glued to the wall you must first ask permission.

Howzat!

◀ **STEP 1**

You will need – cork tiles, marking pen, Stanley knife, steel rule, craft glue, red foam ball about the same size as a cricket ball, white paint and a very fine brush.

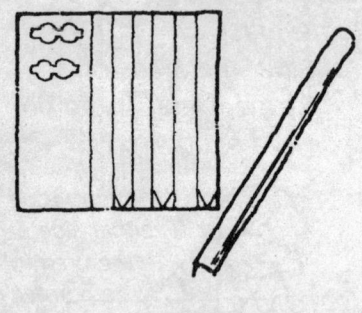

◀ **STEP 2**

Measure the height and width of a real stump, and then mark and cut strips of cork tile to make three stumps. (You will probably need two strips to make one stump of the right height.) Do two tracings of a real bail onto the back of the cork and cut them out.

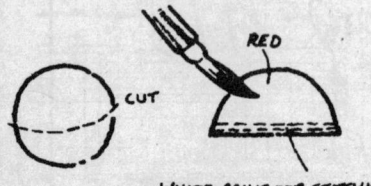

◀ **STEP 3**

Cut the foam ball in half using a large pair of scissors. Carefully paint two rows of close stitching across the ball with the white paint.

Designs on sport

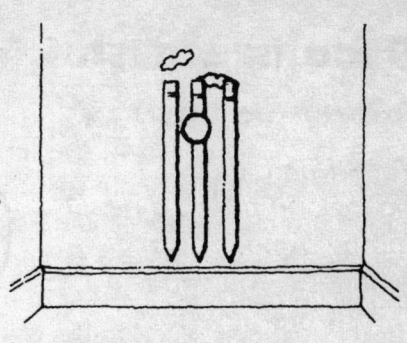

STEP 4
Compose your work of art on the floor, making sure the pieces that make up the stumps join smoothly, and then glue it piece-by-piece onto the wall. Apply a little pressure to make sure the glue adheres.

It's just not cricket

Here's some inspiration for those who want to create wall art for their fave sport. Cork tiles can be used for most of these projects and they can be painted if necessary. Use half a foam ball or circle of cork tile with markings added to make the right ball.

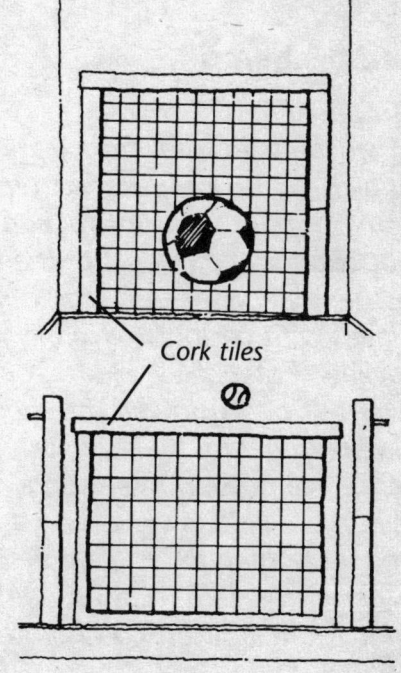

Soccer and hockey – garden netting (either the stiffish plastic type or the soft netting used to cover fruit trees) is fixed to the wall with double-sided tape to create the net.

Tennis – garden netting with a strip of white fabric folded over the top edge is stitched or stapled to make the net.

Deco in a dash

Sporty pin-ups

Target an old darts board and give it a new job by using it as a pinboard. You can leave it as it is or give it a makeover after carefully removing the metal grid. Paint the board in team colours or to resemble a basketball, soccer ball or tennis ball, or cover it with photos of sporting heroes before replacing the grid.

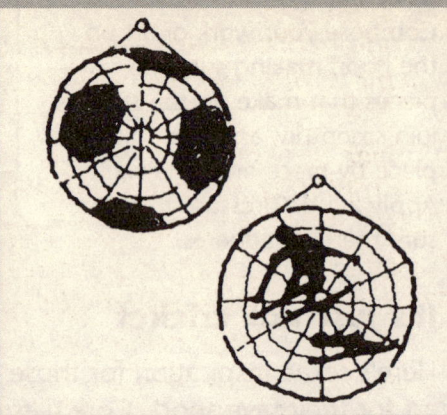

Lamp champ

On pages 76-77 there are instructions for making a leafy papier mâché lampshade. You could use the same instructions, but change the colours of the tissue paper used and replace the leaves with cut-outs of tennis rackets, bats, bikes, blades, or even surfboards! Keep the shapes simple and vary their size to make the pattern interesting. When the light is turned on, you'll see silhouettes of your sporting cut-outs.

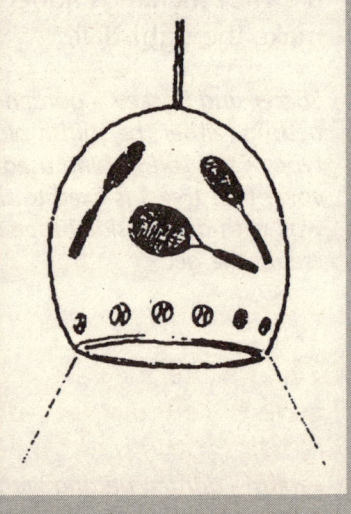

AAGRRH! It is vital that an adult trims the lampshade to match the light fitting and attaches it to the fitting.

Designs on sport

Club colours

On page 41 there's the how-to for making 'Screen stars' using ribbons or strips of fabric. Adapt this to the sports theme by making it in your team or club colours.

To hide the kit under your bed and glam your bed, why not trim it with squares of fabric in team colours. To decorate one long side of a single bed, you'll need five squares of fabric the same size as a man's handkerchief. To cover a short side, about two squares. Before you start cutting, check the height of the bed – you may have to adjust the size of the fabric squares if you have a tall bed. Attach the fabric using a staple gun or double-sided tape.

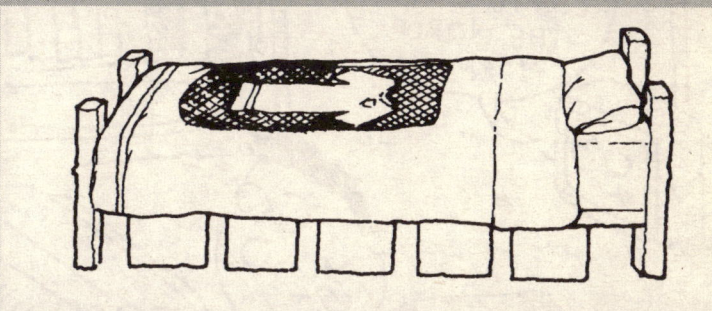

It's a goal!

The ends of the curtain rod have been fitted with two small plastic footballs. A hole is made in the ball, smaller than the rod and then slightly larger cross slits are made with a Stanley knife, allowing the balls to be pushed onto the rod.

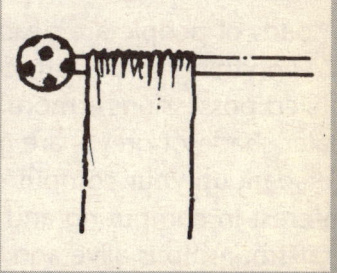

 Computer crazy

Go on, take a byte

Loads of people are dead-keen on anything and everything to do with computers. Understandably, these prized possessions – more often than not boxes that are a paler shade of grey – are given pride of place in their room. To spark up your computer area, show off your huge interest in computing and demonstrate that handmade craftsmanship is alive and well, here's a gigabyte of techno-deco ideas for your room.

Old computers rest home

Many of the ideas in this chapter use bits recycled from <u>very dead, very useless, very much unwanted computers and accessories</u>. Re-read the underlined words because there is no joy to be had in harming working, useful and much-needed gear.

You can often get your hands on old circuit boards, monitors, keyboards, memory chips and computer consumables (disks, for example) by visiting or contacting the following –

Junk shops and car boot sales – you'll have to hand over some dosh to get your hands on the stuff you want.

Recycling centres – computer gear dumped at these places is often purchased by the lorry-load by companies who salvage the useable bits. The useable bits often end up in technology-poor countries where ingenious types, driven by desperate need, cobble the bits together to make working machines. (Recycling centres do deserve their name!) When you approach the manager of a recycling centre and ask if you can take this or that, he or she may say "go ahead, take what you need" or may give you the name of the salvage company.

Computer managers – within large companies there is usually someone who is responsible for buying, maintaining, updating and disposing of computer gear. Find the right, kind-hearted manager and you'll have hit pure silicon!

Newspaper ads – computer salvage companies and techno-fanatics often advertise that they have gear to sell or are looking to buy. Contact them, explain that you're looking for totally-clapped-out, can't-be-repaired stuff and that your pocket money wouldn't cover the cost of a postage stamp.

Computer crazy

What you can do

Here's what you can do to give your bedroom the hip-hop, techno-garage look. You'll find the how-to instructions on pages 60-69.

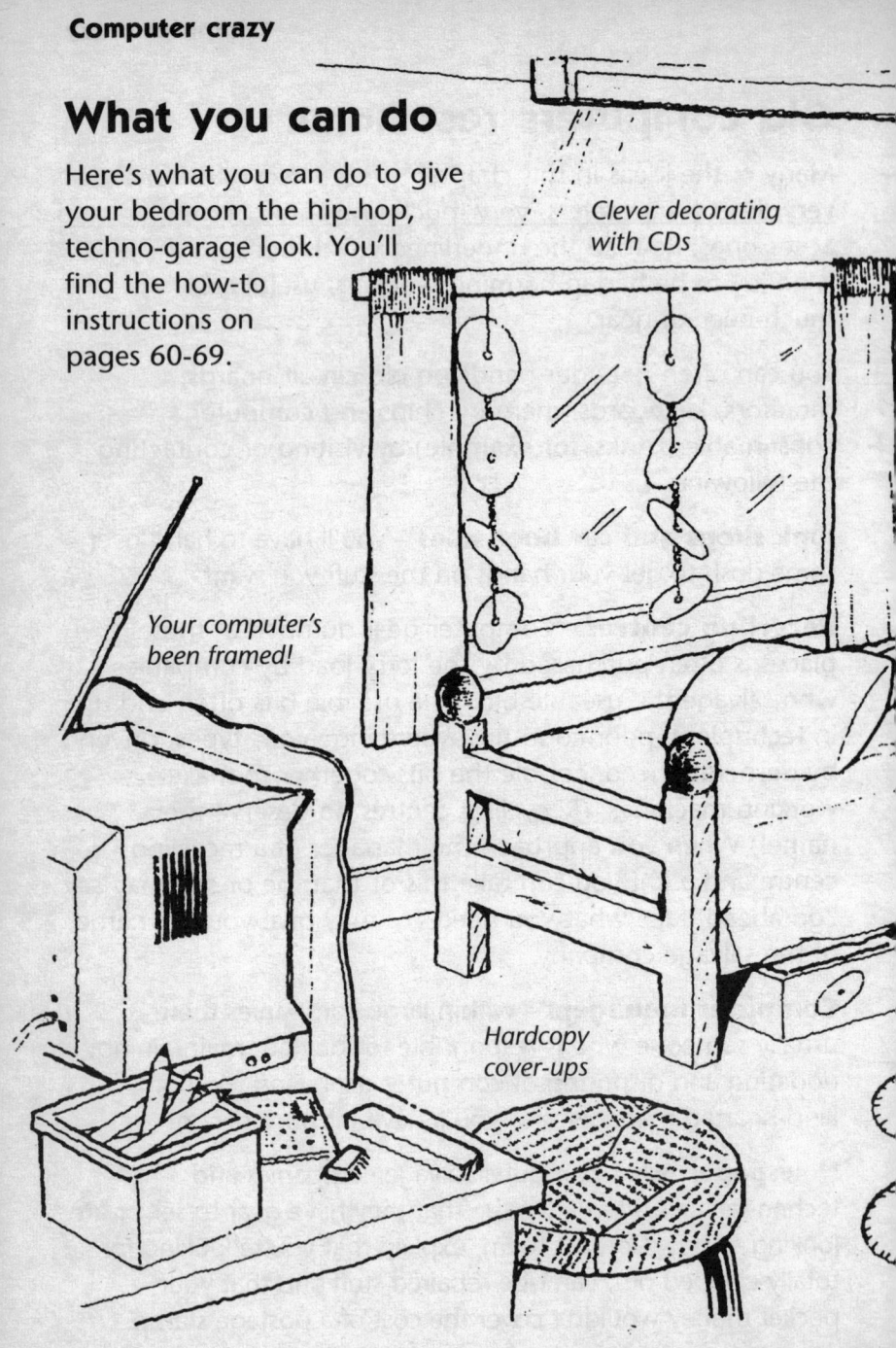

Clever decorating with CDs

Your computer's been framed!

Hardcopy cover-ups

Computer crazy

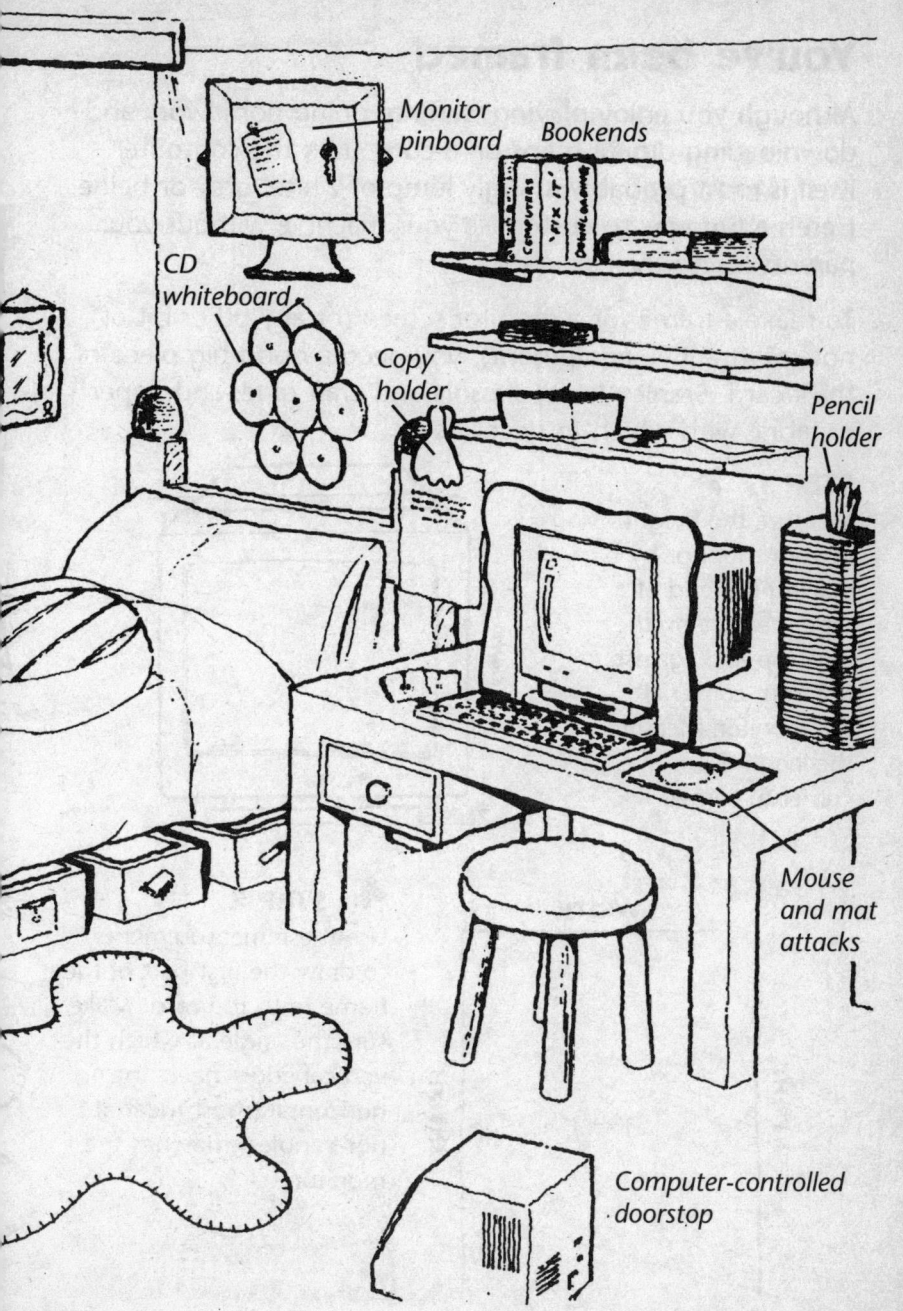

Computer crazy

You've been framed

Although you enjoy playing, surfing, doing homework and downloading digital snaps on a computer, the computer itself is most probably an ugly lump of white, grey or beige. Here's a fun way to customise your machine without your parents losing their pixels.

To make a frame for a monitor screen (or any other bit of not-so-attractive equipment), you need a good big piece of thick card, Stanley knife, scissors and craft glue, and paper or fabric with which to decorate it.

STEP 1

Measure the height of your monitor by placing the end of a tape measure on the desk top and against the front corner of the monitor. Measure the length from corner to corner.

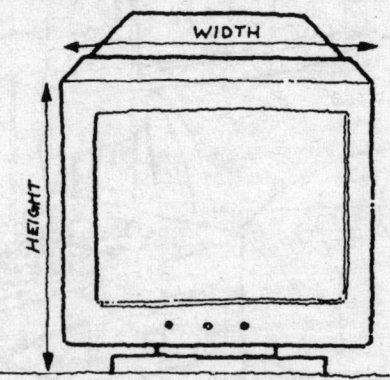

◀ STEP 2

Use these measurements to draw the first part of the frame onto the card. Make sure the angle at which the vertical edge meets the horizontal (most meet at right angles) matches the monitor.

Computer crazy

STEP 3 ▶

Decide on a shape for the outside edge of the frame – straight, wavy or angular, for example, and draw it so that it lies about 8 cm outside the already drawn frame. Mark the frame so you know which side goes to the front.

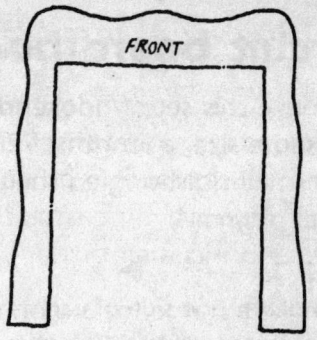

STEP 4 ▶

Draw 2.5 cm to 5 cm tabs on the inside edge of the frame, as shown. These tabs will help hold the frame in place. Use a Stanley knife to cut out the frame.

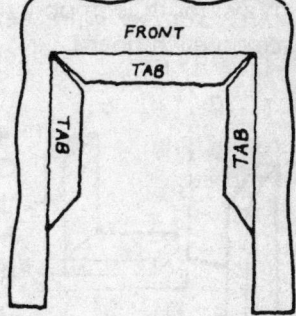

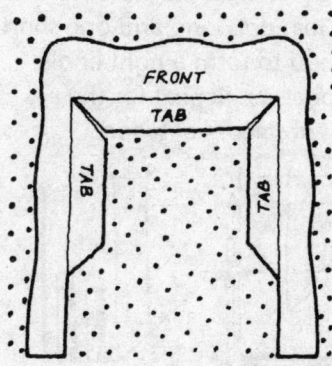

◀ STEP 5

Lay the frame ('front' facing up) onto the right side of the paper or fabric and carefully trace around it. Cut out the paper or fabric then glue it to the 'front' of the frame.

STEP 6 ▶

Gently bend back the tabs and slide the frame onto the monitor. Use blobs of sticky tack (see page 26) to hold the frame in place.

Computer crazy

Circuit board bookends

To make this set of bookends you need two circuit boards the same size, a length of 2.5 cm x 10 cm wood, wood glue, four small right-angled shelf brackets, wood screws and small panel pin nails.

STEP 1 ▶
Strip-down one side of each circuit board, so that you end up with a smooth, component-free face on each board.

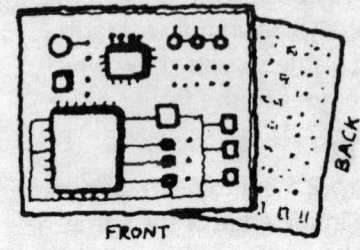

◀ STEP 2
Cut two pieces of wood 2.5 cm shorter than the length of the board, and two pieces 2.5 cm shorter than the width of the board. Join one long and one short piece of wood to form a right angle, and glue together. Repeat for the remaining two pieces of wood.

STEP 3 ▶
Use screws to fit the angle brackets, as shown. Use a bradawl to make starting holes for the screws.

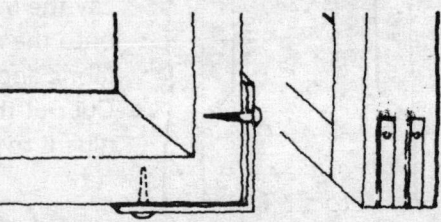

◀ STEP 4
Lay the bookends on their sides and glue on the boards so that they conceal the wooden upright and base of each bookend. Hammer in the nails through the small holes in the boards.

Hardcopy cover-ups

The paperless age has not yet arrived, so here is a way of recycling paper and decorating MDF or wooden shelves and a stool. You can use computer printouts of totally incomprehensible programming instructions, computer-type pictures cut from magazines, or even print out graphics from the Web onto the back of already printed paper.

Shelf life

Ask an adult to remove the shelves off the wall, if possible. It makes this job much easier. Glue the paper randomly (overlapping is fine) onto the top, sides and underside of each shelf so that the MDF or wood is totally covered. Press to make the surface as smooth as possible and wipe away excess glue before it dries. When totally dry, apply two or three coats of clear, matt varnish.

Computer stool

Use the same technique, but to get a smooth finish on a round, wooden stool seat it's best to use smaller pieces of paper or even strips of paper. If you're really enthusiastic, you can paper the legs by winding 5 cm wide strips around the legs and cross bars.

Handy Mandy

Use the same technique to make a musical chair using sheet music, which can be picked up for a song (geddit?) at jumble sales and charity shops.

Computer crazy

The desktop

Rebuild your desktop – not the screen sort, but the flat wooden sort – so that it stays clean and tidy with these very PC ideas.

Pen holder

Floppy disks of the 5.25-inch variety are well and truly old hat, so you should be able to pick up a huge stack of them for nothing. Glue the floppies one on top of the other to form a column about 13 cm high. Spray the column to give it a shiny, metallic finish. When dry, use the hole through the centre of the column to store pens and pencils.

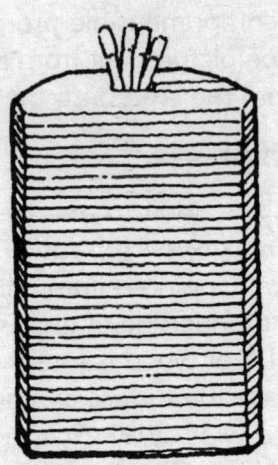

Chip pins!

Use pointy-nosed pliers to remove memory chips from an unwanted circuit board. Fix the chips to flat-headed drawing pins with craft glue and allow to dry before using your chip pins on a pinboard. Make a computer-generation pinboard by adapting the ideas on pages 36-37.

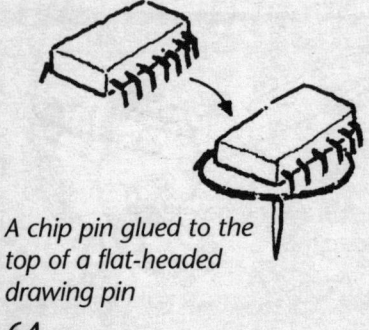

A chip pin glued to the top of a flat-headed drawing pin

Monitor-shaped pinboard

Computer crazy

Hold the front page!

This copy holder, which grips a piece of paper next to your screen, makes doing homework on a computer easier.

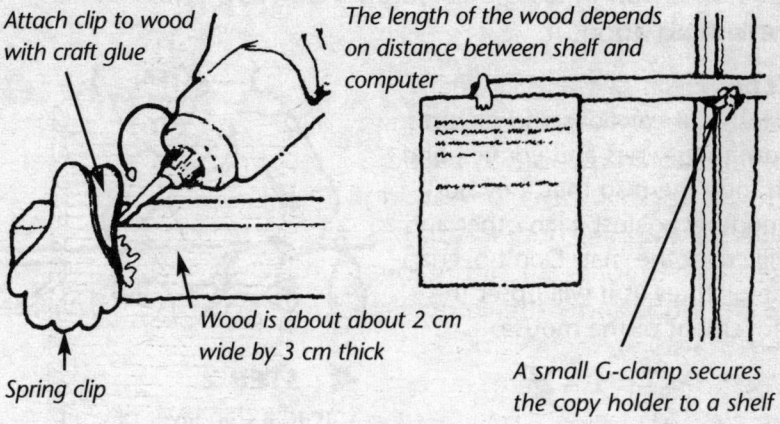

Attach clip to wood with craft glue

The length of the wood depends on distance between shelf and computer

Wood is about about 2 cm wide by 3 cm thick

Spring clip

A small G-clamp secures the copy holder to a shelf

Jazz up your copy holder with silver paint and decorate it with reflective or hologram-type stickers.

Computer-controlled door

Many of the old home computers – Oric, Spectrum and ZX81, for example – were small, wedge-shaped machines that would make perfect doorstops. Prise open the case and pull out and save the innards. Place a couple of hefty stones in the base before closing the case. Decorate the case by spraying it gold or a glow-in-the-dark colour.

A pioneering computer doorstop.

Computer crazy

Mat attack!

Unless you've recently received a fancy mouse mat as a birthday or Christmas present, your mouse most probably rests on a boring, single coloured mat. Here's how to do something about it.

STEP 1 ▶
Neatly cut cartoons and pictures from magazines and comics, and arrange them so that they butt smoothly against each other and will cover the mat. Don't overlap the pictures as it will upset the movement of the mouse.

◀ **STEP 2**
Spread a thin layer of craft glue over the mat and position the pictures, pressing them down – especially the edges – and wiping off any excess glue. Allow to dry.

STEP 3 ▶
Apply two or three coats of clear, matt varnish for a hard, protective finish. If the dried surface is too slippery for the mouse, gently rub over with fine sandpaper. Brush off the dust before you let your mouse loose on the new mat.

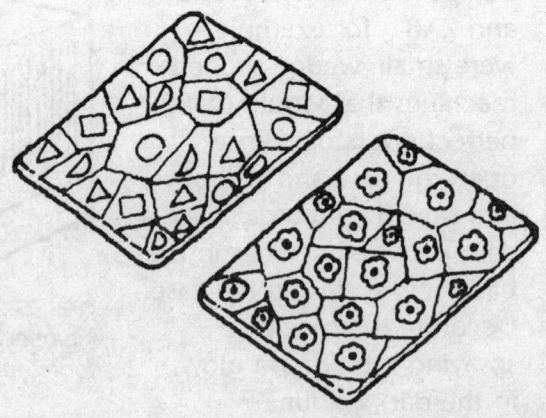

Computer crazy

Is it a mouse?

If you have a spare mouse, then why not consider customising it, too.

All you need is a small piece of spotted or tiger-print furry fabric, scissors, a pair of goo-goo eyes (you can buy these in craft or fabric shops) and double-sided tape.

AAGRRH! Ask an adult to disconnect the mouse from the computer.

Cut the fur fabric so that it covers the top and sides, but not the buttons. Position strips or squares of double-sided tape on the mouse, as shown, then press on the fur fabric. ▼

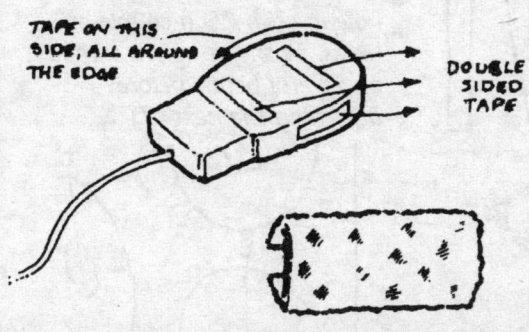

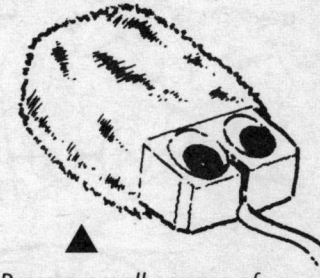

Press a small square of double-sided tape to the back of the goo-goo eyes and position on the mouse.

Handy Mandy

Whatever you do, make sure that nothing interferes with the mouse's movement, tail (the lead connecting it to the computer) or buttons. Don't use runny paints, glue or varnish because they jam up the button and the chemicals in these products can play havoc with the casing and internal works.

Computer crazy

CD stands for clever decorating!

Never throw away rubbishy, freebie, give-away, clapped-out CDs ever again because here are two mega decorating ideas that you will want to do. You'll be so impressed with the CD window screen and CD whiteboard that you'll be hounding everyone you know to hand-over their unwanted CDs.

Blinded by the light

You will need a great stack of CDs, nylon fishing line and some eye-catching beads.

Knot one end of a long, long length of nylon line to a table leg. This will prevent tangles. Thread the line through the hole in each CD a couple of times, as shown. Then thread on several beads before attaching the next CD.

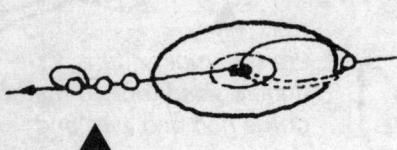

It's a good idea to tie a knot after each CD and string of beads

When a 'line' is long enough, firmly knot the end. Cut the line away from the table leg and hang your CD screen from an existing curtain rail or from a length of dowelling. Make as many 'lines' as you need to decorate or fill a window.

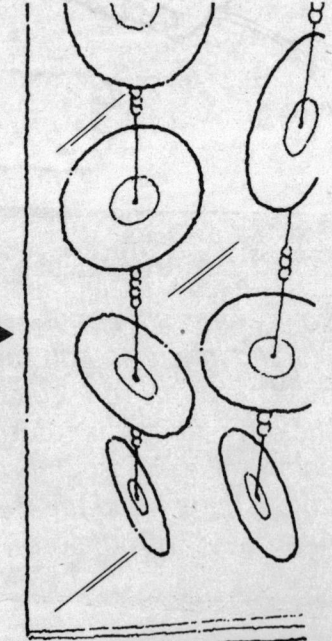

Erasable disks

The shiny side of a CD works in the same way as an expensive whiteboard. Write on your message using a special dry-board marker, and then wipe it off with a cloth or paper towel.

To make a CD message board you will need seven to ten unwanted CDs; a large piece of thick, white card; craft glue; and Stanley knife.

STEP 1 ▶
Arrange the CDs on the card into a square, triangle or circle. Space the CDs evenly and try to get them as close to each other as possible without any overlapping. Glue the CDs, shiny-side up, to the card. Press them firmly in place.

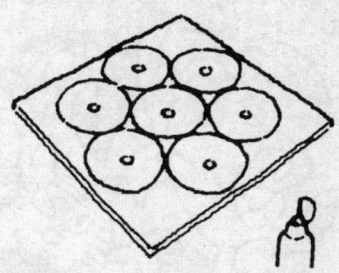

STEP 2 ▶
Use the knife to cut away excess card from around your whiteboard. Fix the whiteboard to a wall or to the back of a door, using double-sided tape or pads.

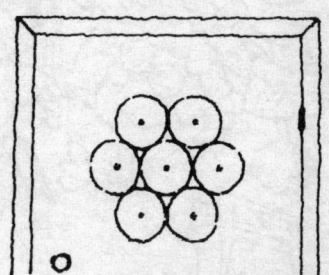

Handy Mandy

CDs are really useful things, here are some more compact ideas –

- *Backed with felt, which is fixed on with craft glue, CDs make great drinks coasters.*
- *Use plain or painted ones to decorate a wall in your room.*

6 The great outdoors... indoors!

Revamping, naturally

If you like the great outdoors and love plants and wildlife, there are ideas aplenty – all inspired by nature's bounty – in this chapter for the eco warrior.

You can choose to revamp your room so that it looks like a jungle, a botanical garden, a desert or a room in a museum of natural history. What you do depends on your particular interest, your imagination and what is possible within the confines of your room. But while 'looks' are all important, revamping naturally also means trying to use materials and products that are environmentally friendly.

The great outdoors . . . indoors!

Not costing the Earth

Most of the projects in this book look to be seriously eco-friendly by using up something that would otherwise have ended up in a rubbish bin. There's a lot to know about the whole saving-the-planet-caper, but if you can recycle even 10 items that's 10 less things that end up on a landfill site and 10 less things that have to be manufactured.

An environmentally friendly product is manufactured without damaging the environment, and can be used without causing you ill effects.

When buying DIY materials, always check to see if the manufacturers claim that their product is 'environmentally friendly'. If you are not sure, then write to the manufacturer.

Handy Mandy

Fill your room with the sounds of nature by recording bird song, chirruping crickets, whistling wind and crashing waves. If you go to a zoo, you can record really wild sounds!

The great outdoors . . . indoors!

What you can do

The eco-instructions for these ideas are on pages 74-85.

Hang out with a twig rig

Zebra-print curtains

Decorated plant pots

The two-faced pinboard

Tanks for the cacti

Drip vase

Busy bee stool

The great outdoors . . . indoors!

The great outdoors . . . indoors!

Keeping track

Whatever your dates with nature – a young eco-campaigners' meeting, horse-riding, bird-watching – keep track of them with this combined clipboard and blackboard. One half is a blackboard; the other, a clipboard. You can make the board as large as you like, but we found that one 50 cm by 80 cm was the most useful.

AAGRRH! MDF is a heavy material, so ask an adult to help you fix the board securely onto a wall.

You will need a piece of MDF, two wooden battens the width of the MDF, wood glue, wood screws, blackboard paint, emulsion paint, paintbrush and a large bulldog clip.

Design ideas

Simply dotty! *Paw prints*

Leaf shapes *Flower power*

The great outdoors . . . indoors!

STEP 1 ▶
Glue a batten along the top and the bottom edges of the front of the board. Then firmly attach the batten with screws top and bottom.

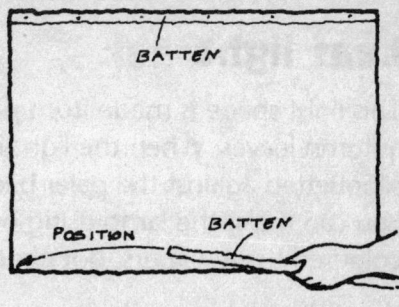

◀ STEP 2
Rough out your design on paper, remembering that one half should be left blank for the blackboard. Use a lead pencil to transfer your design onto the board.

STEP 3 ▶
Use emulsion paint to paint your design, always applying the lightest colours first. Allow to dry between coats and before painting the other half with blackboard paint. Three coats of blackboard paint may be necessary.

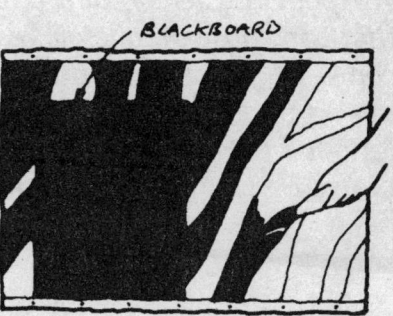

◀ STEP 4
Use a screw to fix the bulldog clip into the batten on the decorated half of the board. Store sticks of chalk and pens on the batten along the bottom of the board.

75

The great outdoors . . . indoors!

Leaf light

This light shade is made from papier mâché and dried autumn leaves. When the light is switched on, the leaves are silhouetted against the paler background – it looks stunning! You can make the lamp using one or a combination of coloured tissue papers, but choose pale not dark colours.

You will need – a balloon; string; lots of white, cream, yellow, silver or gold tissue paper; a selection of flat, dry leaves (the more interesting the shapes, the better); a small packet of wallpaper paste and a mixing container and spoon; rubber gloves; and a brush for applying paste.

Handy Mandy   AAGRRH!

Wallpaper paste contains a fungicide that can cause an allergic reaction if it comes in contact with the skin. When mixing or applying wallpaper paste, ask for adult help and wear rubber clothes, protective clothing and goggles.

STEP 1 ▶

Inflate the balloon and seal with tightly-knotted string. Place the knotted-end of the balloon in a container. Put on the rubber gloves and mix up the wallpaper paste following the instructions on the packet.

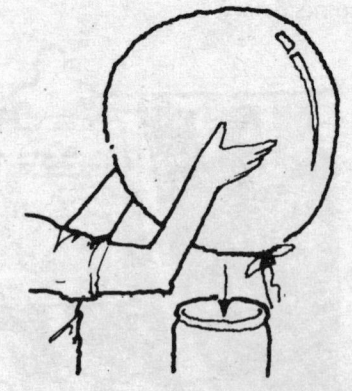

The great outdoors . . . indoors!

STEP 2 ▶

Tear the tissue into strips roughly 7 cm by 15 cm. Place a strip of tissue on the balloon and brush over with paste. Repeat to cover the balloon (leave the lower quarter uncovered) with two layers of tissue.

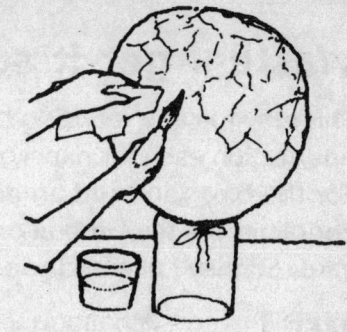

◀ **STEP 3**

Use the paste to glue leaves around the shade, then paste on two more layers of tissue. Leave to dry for two to three days.

STEP 5 ▶

Untie the string and gradually let the air out of the balloon. Pull the balloon out, making sure no bits are left behind. Use small, sharp scissors to neaten the edge of the shade.

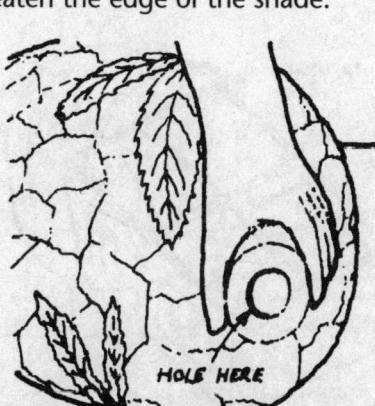

HOLE HERE

◀ **STEP 5** AAGRRH!

Cut a hole the same size as the light fitting (ask an adult to help you) in the top of the shade. Cut two rings of card to fit neatly around the hole for the light fitting. Glue them around the holes – one on the inside of the shade, the other on the outside. Ask an adult to fit the shade onto the light fitting.

The great outdoors . . . indoors!

Waste – get it sorted!

This easy-to-carry recycling bin is divided into four sections, one section each for paper, cans, cardboard and bottles. For the bin, you need an old plastic laundry basket or a container made of metal or wood. You will also need thick card, Stanley knife and rope.

STEP 1 ▶

Cut one piece of card the same width and depth of the container, another that is the same length and depth of the container. Write 'bottom' along the edges that fit against the base of the container.

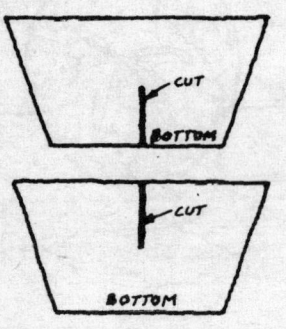

◀ STEP 2

In one piece of card, cut a slot from the middle of the 'bottom' edge to halfway across. Repeat for the other card, but start the cut from the unmarked (top) edge.

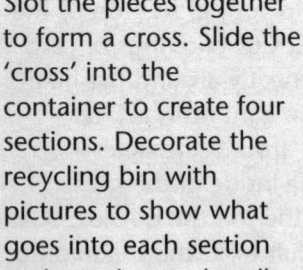

STEP 3 ▶

Slot the pieces together to form a cross. Slide the 'cross' into the container to create four sections. Decorate the recycling bin with pictures to show what goes into each section and attach rope handles.

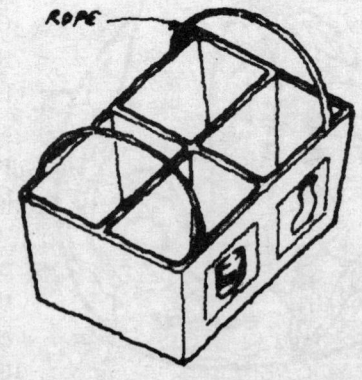

Snake charmer

This snake is an all-weather best friend. In winter, put him in front of a door to keep warm air in and cold air out. In summer, this snake will hold the door open so that you can catch nature's cooling breeze.

You will need hardwearing fabric or fur fabric; sewing thread and needle; an old pair of tights; clean, dry sand; red felt; and a pair of goo-goo eyes or two buttons.

STEP 1
Draw the pattern onto the wrong side of the fabric, then cut it out.

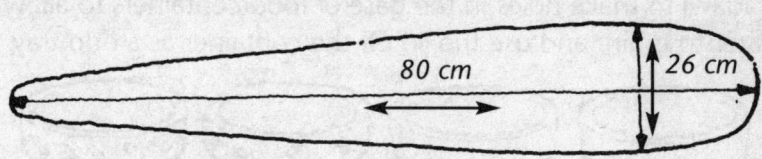

STEP 2
Pin the fabric, wrong sides facing together, and stitch from tail and along the body using a backstitch. Leave the head open, and turn the fabric right way out.

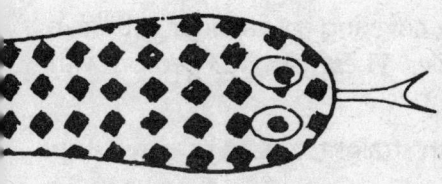

STEP 3
Cut one leg off the tights and fill it with 6 to 8 cups of sand. Tightly close the end with a rubber band. Stuff the sand-filled tight inside the fabric tube, spreading the sand so that it fills the tube evenly. Close the opening with more stitches.

Attach a forked tongue and button or goo-goo eyes, and the snake charmer who makes draughts hissss-tory is finished.

The great outdoors . . . indoors!

Plant power

Pots of well-tended plants are great decorating tools and really bring the outdoors indoors! We'll leave the choice of plants up to you (scented herbs love a warm spot on a sunny window sill), but check that they are indoor plants and then make sure you tend them well. Because all homes are full of dust, wipe the leaves to remove dust so that the plant can breathe.

Raising the standard

Here are some ways of transforming the standard plastic plant pot and large ice cream, butter and yoghurt containers. Use a bradawl to make holes in the base of food containers to allow water to drain, and use the lid off the container as a drip tray.

 Paint a container with emulsion or gloss paint. When dry, apply craft glue and sprinkle over with glitter or sand to create a textured pattern.

 Glue pea sticks or bamboo canes to the side of a container, then tie strands of twine around the container for a Japanese-inspired look.

 Get the bejewelled look by covering a container with fake gems, buttons or mosaic tiles. These can be fixed on with craft glue.

 Decorate the container with straight, zigzag or wavy strips of sticky-back plastic.

 Use a sponge to dab the container with two shades of paint to give a mottled finish.

You drip!

You can use the drip technique to decorate all types and shapes of containers, but it's most effective on tall bottles, which can be used as vases for cut or dried flowers.

You will need a container, pot, jar or bottle; thick emulsion or gloss paint; lots of newspaper; and an unwanted spoon.

Turn the container upside-down on newspaper. (A funnel or two bricks will support an upturned bottle.) Spoon paint onto the base and push it over the edge to let the paint run slowly down the bottle. Allow to dry.

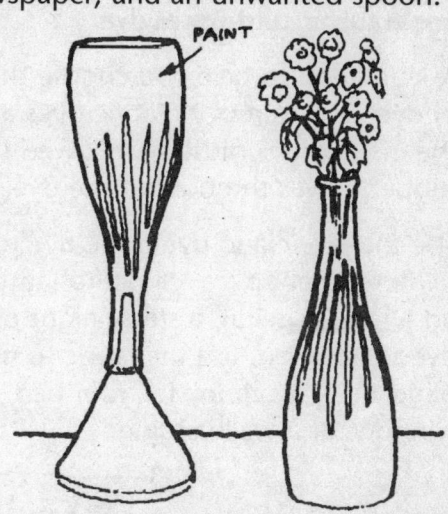

Greenfinger tips

1 Plant pots should be empty and clean before painting. Allow to dry and air before planting.

2 Cover the soil or compost in the plant pots with gravel, pebbles, smooth glass beads, marbles, seashells, moss or pieces of bark as they will help the soil retain moisture.

3 Arrange dried flowers in bottles filled with clean, dry sand (see page 84 for how to make coloured sand) or gravel.

The great outdoors . . . indoors!

To dye for

Not many households have loads of unwanted cotton fabric, and even rarer – fabric in exactly the colour or print you want. So, what is the solution? Keep your eyes peeled at jumble sales and charity shops for plain sheets, curtains and curtain linings, and then buy pots or packets of fabric dye, preferably a cold-water dye.

Ask an adult to help you choose the right type and quantity of dye, and to mix it. Fabric dyes are powerful, which is why the instructions must be followed to the letter. Always wear rubber gloves throughout the dyeing process.

Use the fabric and dye to tie-dye patterns that resemble a rainforest canopy, a 'carpet' of autumn leaf colours, ripples on a lake, the Sun, a starry night or an animal print. Once dyed and dried, use the fabric to make a room divider (see page 111), a canopy for your bed, a screen for a door or window, or a wallhanging.

Different methods of tying the fabric before dyeing will create radiating ripples or stripes.

The great outdoors . . . indoors!

All tied up

The sections of fabric that are bound with strong, wide rubber bands; string or twine; or knotted do not absorb the dye. So if the fabric is yellow and you use a dark blue dye, the tied sections will remain yellow. Following are four ways of 'tying' the fabric to create different tie-dye patterns.

Stars and circles – rubber bands wound on tightly to completely cover a very small section of fabric. To create larger areas of undyed fabric, increase the amount of fabric bound by wide rubber bands.

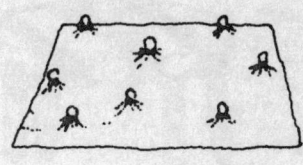

Ripples – find the centre of the fabric and 'fold' it to look like a closed umbrella. Use wide rubber bands to tie it, as shown. Gradually increase the spacing between each tie.

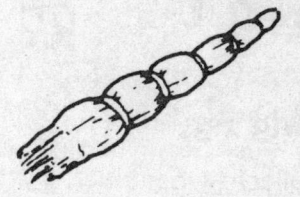

Stripes – roll, twist, scrunch or concertina-fold the fabric, and bind it by winding round string and knotting. The wider the binding, the wider the undyed stripe.

Splodges – to create a random pattern that could resemble clouds racing across a sky or a rainforest canopy, tie the fabric in knots as well as tying with strings and rubber bands.

Handy Mandy

To keep in with the natural theme, suspend tie-dyed screens or curtains from bamboo canes. While dyeing the fabric, dye some string or twine in the same colour. This can be used to tie back the curtain or screen, decorate plant pots or to make a Twig Rig (see page 84).

The great outdoors . . . indoors!

Deco in a dash

Fur-niture

Fun fur in animal-print designs can be used to cover lots of surfaces in your room. Check out the fur stool on pages 34-35, or the cosy-toes rug on page 41.

◄ *Create a buzz by covering a stool with stripy black and yellow fur fabric.*

Twig rig

Collect twigs, driftwood, feathers, shells, pebbles and leaves, and link them with twine to create a wall decoration.

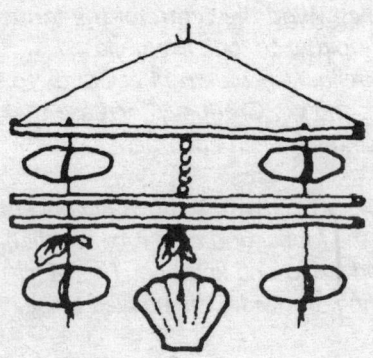

Sands of lime

Use coloured sand to support dried flower arrangements or to create sand paintings. All you need is clean, fine-grain sand and a bottle of food colouring. Half-fill a plastic container with sand and then pour in water to cover the sand. Drop in food colouring until you get the strength of colour you're after. (Less colouring makes for a pale shade.) Stir the mixture well and leave to settle for 30 to 40 minutes. Carefully pour off the water, then spoon the sand onto paper towels laid over sheets of newspaper. Spread the sand out and leave to dry on a sunny window sill.

The great outdoors . . . indoors!

The collector

Sometimes the simplest things can be used to make striking decorations. See if these ideas can find space in your room –

- Piles of smooth pebbles.

- Clear, glass jars filled with layers of coloured sand, gravel and shells.

- An unwanted fish tank can be given a new job as a gravel-lined home for cacti.

- Glue one or two interesting natural objects on a piece of roughly cut styrofoam (or three layers of thick card glued together), and then paint entirely white or cream to look like the plaster casts taken by geologists.

- Use interestingly-shaped leaves as stencils or cut your own designs, and paint or spray-paint around them to decorate furniture, lampshades and fabric.

Fright night

There may come a time when a parent just says no to major style-surgery on your room. That time might come when you ask to paint your bedroom black to give it the full chamber of horror look. But don't worry, this chapter is brimming with loads of other spine-chillingly haunting ideas!

Handy Mandy

If you are having a Halloween party use the quick and inexpensive ideas in this chapter to decorate your home and set the spooky atmosphere. Creepy-crawlies stuck to your front door with sticky tack, for example, are bound to get the party off to a howling start!

Fright night

Purple – the new black

If you've given up trying for total black, perhaps you could compromise using a dark blue (midnight blue sounds spookier) or deep purple. These colours look almost proper, even human, in daylight, but at night, they're as creepy as black.

You don't have to go for four walls and ceiling coverage, you could do one wall in a dark colour (sometimes called a feature wall) and then 'decorate' the rest of the room with spooky wallhangings, spider webs, masks and other scary objects.

Bargain basement

The best time to look for inexpensive 'fright night' props is in the days just after Halloween (All Hallows Eve) on October 31. Large and small shops don't have the room to store unsold plastic pitchforks, blood-shot eyeballs, rubber creepy-crawlies, masks, witches' hats, and other Halloween paraphernalia, so they sell it off cheaply. This is when you strike, stretching your pocket money as far as it will go.

Once you have a stockpile of ghoulish props, you can use them as they are – a pitchfork hatstand would be  very practical – or use your creativity to make them more macabre. Eyeball or creepy-crawly paperweights are must-haves!

Fright night

What you can do

This is how your dungeon of doom could look if you follow the instructions on pages 90-97.

It's curtains for you

Shock therapy

Fright night

Fright night

Creepy wallhanging

You can make this paper wallhanging any size you like, and all you need is a roll or large sheet of black sugarpaper, a stick of white chalk, scissors, white paper, glow-in-the-dark (luminous) water-based paints and brush, sticky tape, and dowelling or a bamboo cane.

◀ STEP 1
Cut the sugarpaper to the length you want. Spread it out on the floor or work surface and use white chalk to draw pairs of sneaky, creepy eyes. Don't forget to draw in the pupils.

STEP 2 ▶
Cut out the eye shapes, but not the pupils. (I hope this isn't too gory for you.) Then, paint pieces of paper in luminous colours to put behind the 'eye holes'. Leave to dry thoroughly.

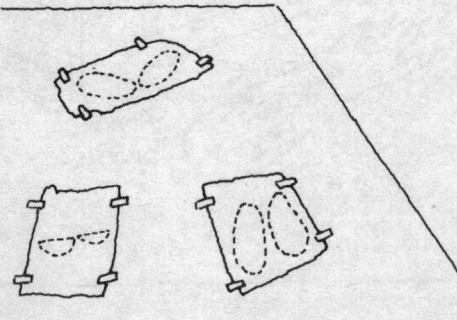

◀ STEP 3
Cut the painted papers into pieces larger than the eye holes they will cover. Sticky tape them, painted side down, over the eye holes.

Fright night

STEP 4

Place the dowelling or bamboo cane across the top and roll the paper over it. Ask someone to hold the paper in place while you secure with a long length of tape.

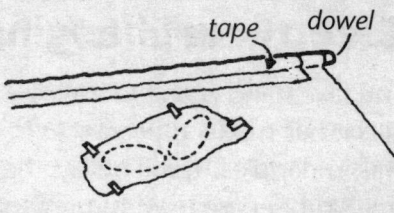

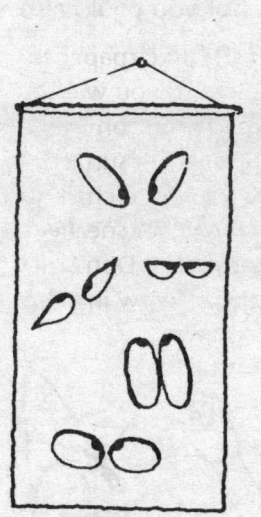

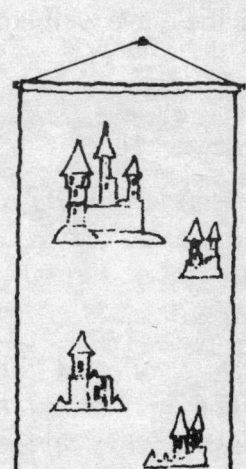

Turn your wallhanging over, attach a length of cord to the ends of the dowelling, and suspend it from a hook on a wall. Try other creepy designs like castles, bats and spiders.

Handy Mandy

Glow-in-the-dark green, yellow or orange paint can be bought in tiny, inexpensive tins from many craft and DIY shops. If you're struggling to lay your hands on a tiny tin of luminous paint, try a fishing shop – anglers use it to make their floats show up in the dark.

Fright night

Give them a big hand

The fake hand is one of the oldest special effects and it has made appearances in every horror film since Dracula was in nappies. Traditionally, the fake hand is made by filling a small rubber glove with runny plaster of Paris, then peeling away the glove once the plaster has set. This is a perfectly good technique if you have plaster of Paris but you could also fill the glove with tightly-crumpled balls of newspaper.

Finger tip!

Instead of gluing cardboard nails onto a fake paper-filled hand, you can instead use fake plastic nails that fit onto the top of your fingers. Packs of these are always on the sale tables after Halloween.

Before you start filling the glove, ask a friend to put on the glove pushing their fingers into the ends. Choose the five largest fake nails and apply craft glue to the inside of the nails and to the glove. Position the fake nails and allow the glue to dry before your friend removes the glove.

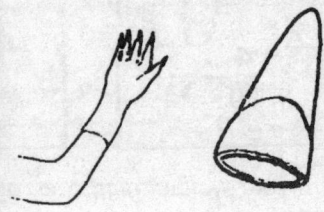

Who would have believed that Dracula wore falsies!

It's coming to get you!

For this hand-bursting-through-a-wall special effect, you will need a small rubber glove, dowelling and matching cup bracket, newspaper, emulsion or luminous paint, red card, craft glue and felt-tip pen.

Fright night

STEP 1
Pack the tip of the middle finger with balls of newspaper, then insert dowelling or bamboo cane (about 2.5 cm/1 in longer than the glove) into the middle finger.

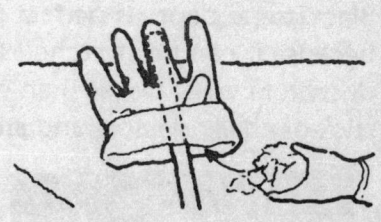

STEP 2
Roll down the top of the glove and pack small balls of newspaper into the fingers of the glove, then fill the palm and wrist.

STEP 3
To seal the end, push thick wads of paper inside the glove to make a stopper for the paper packing. Mould the hand to make it look realistic.

STEP 4
Tie string around the wrist and suspend the glove over sheets of newspaper before painting it white, black or luminous green. When dry, paint the end red. Draw five long fingernails on red card, cut out and stick to the fingertips with craft glue.

STEP 5
Ask an adult to screw a cup bracket the same size as the dowelling onto a wall or wardrobe. To make it look as though the hand is bursting through the wall or door, draw long shatter lines around the bracket with a felt-tip pen.

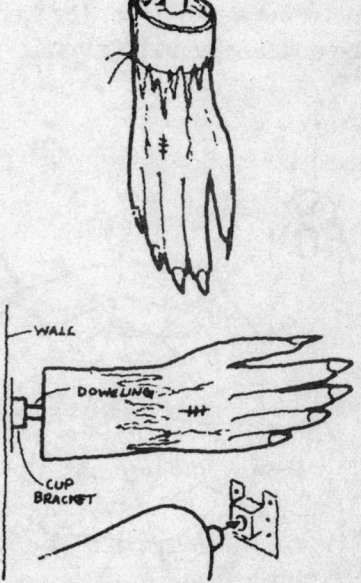

Fright night

WWW – World Weird Web

Black crêpe paper is perfect for making a giant spider's web because it can be stretched to mimic the saggy-look of a dusty, old web. Other than crêpe paper, all you need is a stick of chalk, scissors and sticky tack.

◀ **STEP 1**
Lay the crêpe paper on a smooth surface and use chalk to draw a web using thick lines.

STEP 2
Cut either side of the chalk lines and never cut across a line. The web will be quite flimsy, so be careful.

◀ **STEP 3**
Gently stretch the crêpe paper web before using blobs of sticky tack to attach each arm of the web to the wall.

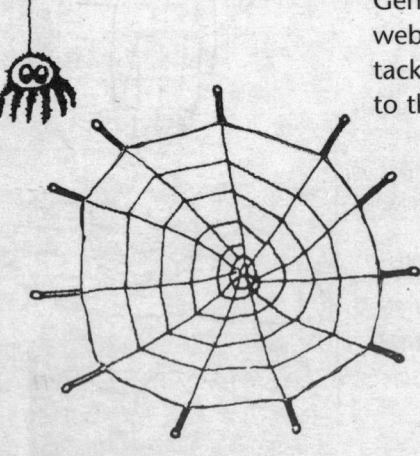

Fright night

Welcome, my pretties . . .

No ghoulish room would be complete without some gruesome insect friends to keep you company. What you need is a pack of rubber or plastic spiders, worms, flies and other six- and eight-legged wriggly things, and double-sided tape, sticky tack or craft glue to fix them in place.

The critters can be stuck wherever you want, adding a delightfully diabolical touch to the least scary of everyday objects such as bookends, shelves, door and drawer knobs, mirrors, curtain poles, windows, lamps and light shades.

Creepy-crawlies add extra fright-value to your room.

Enter at your peril

You'd be more cruel than Professor Frankenstein if you didn't want to give visitors warning of the perils that lay behind the door to your room. Make a warning sign on card, using drip-style lettering that is easy to do by hand. Mount near your sign a Halloween face mask.

If your dressing-up box yields only a clown mask or something else disgustingly cheerful, disguise it by gluing on strips of bandage. Bye, bye Mikey the Clown – enter The Mummy.

Fright night

Dreaded deco in a dash

Sandman

Fill a rubber glove with clean, dry sand to make a paperweight or doorstop. Don't overfill the glove or it will be hard to mould it into a realistic shape. Seal the end tightly with a strong rubber band and knotted string.

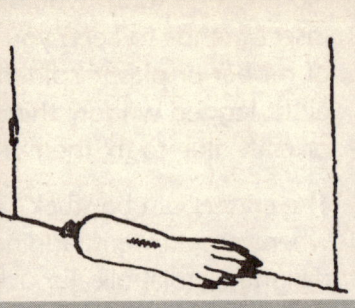

A very handy doorstop.

Shock therapy

So that you can find plugs and sockets in the dark, paint ghoulish images on the back of UNPLUGGED (repeat: unplugged) electrical plugs using glow-in-the dark paints. You only get one chance, so practise your design on paper first.

This frame has been cut with a zig-zag edge and decorated with skulls and flashes of lightning.

◀ Give light switches the shock treatment by painting frames, cut from card, which will fit neatly around the mounting plate. Fix the frames to the wall with double-sided tape or small blobs of sticky tack.

Sounds horrible

Go for the full-on, spine-tingling atmosphere by secretly recording lots of spooky sounds – wolves howling, wind whistling, chains a'rattling and doors creaking – onto a cassette tape. You could even record some dialogue and sound effects from a horror film when it is shown on TV. Conceal your tape player and play your recording when friends come to visit.

Clamped in irons

For the irons or manacles, you need a pair of ultra-cheap, plastic towel holders that consist of a hoop fitted to a mounting. Give them a coat of metallic paint or matt black emulsion, and highlight with red-brown paint for rust. Use double-sided tape or pads to fix them shoulder-width apart onto a wall.

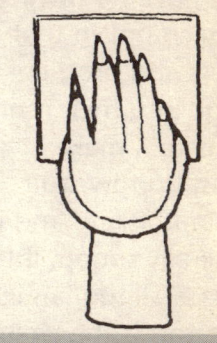

A fake hand (see page 92) slipped through one of the manacles is just too ghoulish for words!

It's curtains for you

What you need is a piece of black fabric or black crêpe paper that will cover a window in your room. Cut it into wide, even, vertical strips leaving 15 cm (6 in) uncut across the top. Decorate the strips with sneaky, creepy eyes, which can be done using luminous paint, fabric paint or pieces of felt. Fix the screen to the window by looping it over an existing curtain rod and pinning or stapling in place.

Top secret

If you've ever read the letters page of teen magazines, you'll have noticed that lots of letter-writers moan that they have no privacy. They complain that sisters and brothers barge into their room uninvited, make a mess, borrow stuff without asking and just generally snoop. If this sounds all too familiar, then this is the chapter for you! There are ideas for scaring off unwanted visitors and some neat ways to conceal private things like your diary from prying eyes. Flip through the other chapters for ways of screening doors and windows, and making a room divider.

Invisible to the naked eye

Unlike all the other revamp ideas in this book that are meant to stand out and be noticed, top secret projects require the hush-hush approach. Carry out the construction in secret so that siblings don't have a clue about what you're doing. When you're ready to install your device, do it quietly and make sure that it can't be spotted. There's no use having a secret compartment inside a drawer if it can be seen the moment the drawer is opened.

Top secret

Keep out . . . please

So that brothers or sisters know they are not welcome in your room without an invitation, it's only right to give fair warning. A sign on the door of your room is the best way to do this, but for it to be taken seriously it has to look the business.

This door poster shows a picture of the nosey sister or brother peering through prison bars. All you need to make the poster is a piece of card, an enlarged photocopy of a photo of the 'snooper', glue and black paper.

Photocopy glued to a piece of card

Lettering done by hand, with stencils or with computer-generated typefaces

Strips of black paper glued over the image to form the prison bars

Handy Mandy

There's one thing to understand about privacy – everyone deserves it! You can't expect a brother or sister to respect your privacy if you're acting like James Bond and snooping around their rooms the moment their backs are turned.

Top secret

Book-er prize

I love this secret space idea and it's the perfect place to hide a small diary, letters, sweets or pocket money. Other than an unwanted hardback book (the thicker, the better) a Stanley knife and glue, all you need is patience. It can take quite a bit of time to cut a hollow through the centre of the pages of the book.

If you can't find a suitable, unwanted book around your home, then check out the 'books for sale' table at your local library or charity shop. Amongst the 10-year-old annuals and the dog-eared romances are bound to be some of the heaviest and thickest books ever on law, chemistry, metaphysics, snail-breeding and other gripping subjects. Once you've chosen a suitably thick tome, make sure that the spine is in good nick and that the pages aren't coming away.

STEP 1 ▶

Open the book – don't worry, you're not going to have to read a single word – and turn over 10 or so pages. Use a ruler and pencil to draw a large rectangle in the middle of the page, leaving a ruler-width border around the edge.

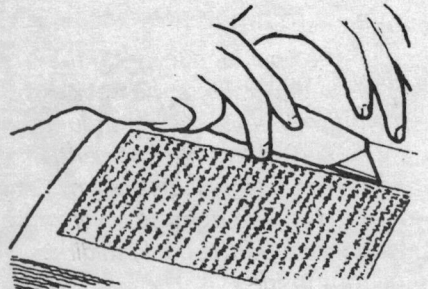

◀ **STEP 2**

Use a metal rule and Stanley knife to cut out the rectangle from the top page and the next 10 to 15 pages in one go.

Top secret

STEP 3 ▶

Keep cutting out the rectangle using the hollowed section as a guide until there are only 10 to 15 pages left in the book.

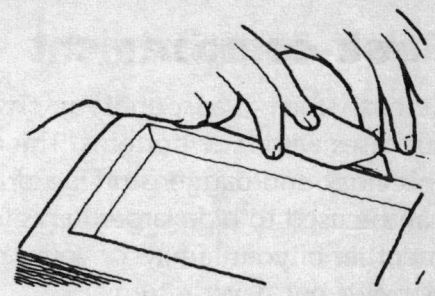

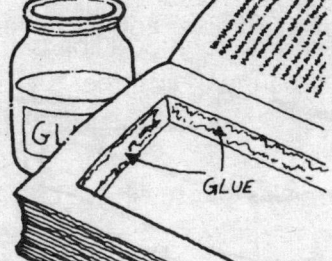

◀ STEP 4

To create a secure hidey-hole for your keepsakes, glue the edges of the hollowed-out pages together, then glue the uncut pages at the beginning and end of the book to each other and to the inside of the cover. Allow to dry thoroughly.

STEP 5 ▶

Drop your diary or pocket money into the hollow, close the book and then slide it among the other books on your shelves.

Cunning disguise

If you're worried that a thick, plain-covered, hardback book will stand out from your real books, cover it using the cartoon, sporting or fashion pages from a newspaper.

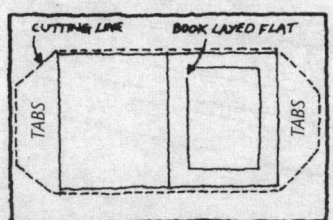

Open the book and lay it on the covering paper. Press the book down firmly while tracing around the book. Remove the book and draw generous tabs, as shown. Cut out the cunning disguise cover and wrap it around the book, folding the tabs inside.

Top secret

False compartment

To hide stolen plans, photographs and films, spies always had suitcases with false bottoms. The bedroom equivalent to all this cloak-and-dagger stuff is a drawer with a false back that can be used to hide larger items like a birthday present for a member of your family, or your favourite CD that everyone borrows but never returns.

All you need is a drawer (size doesn't matter), a piece of stiff card the same colour as the inside of the drawer and sticky tape.

STEP 1 ▶
Measure the inside width and height of the drawer. Use these measurements to draw a square or rectangle onto the card. Draw tabs onto the side and bottom edges of the square or rectangle.

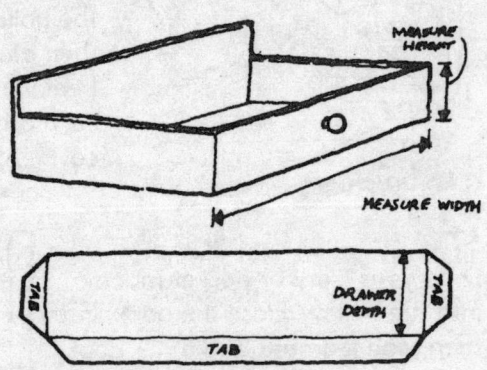

STEP 2 ▶
Cut out the card and fold back the tabs. Insert the card into the drawer (tabs towards the back of the drawer) and fix with sticky tape. Viewed from most angles, it will look as though the card marks the end of the drawer, but behind it there's a secret space for storage.

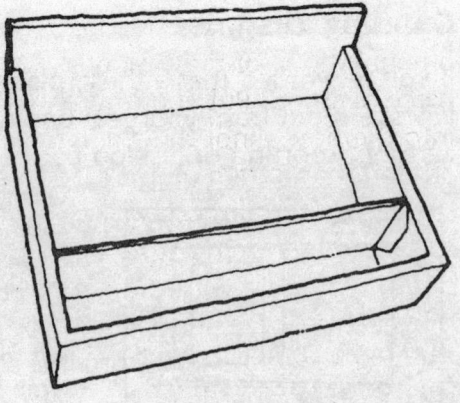

Top secret

Three secret sites

Shh, it's behind you
Get hold of one or two fruit bags – the type that oranges are sold in – and a couple of small suction hooks or self-adhesive hooks. Press the hooks onto the back of your bedhead and then hook on the fruit bags. Use the fruit bags to store sweets for a midnight treat. Naughty, but nice.

Shh, it's under you
A small, plastic container with a snap-on lid can make a fab secret store underneath a table or chair. Fix the lid of the container carefully onto the bottom of the chair with craft glue. When dry, snap on the base of the container. Use this hideaway for lightweight items.

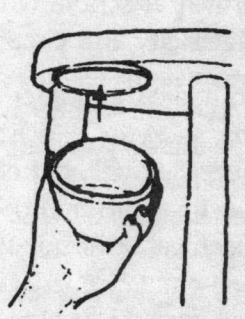

Shh, it's above you
This secret store is not easy to get to, so it's a great place to hide money if you're saving up for something. All you need is one leg (cut at knee height) off an old pair of tights and a piece of string. Put your money into the tight, knot the string around it and then tie the string to a curtain rod. Make sure that your secret store doesn't interfere with the movement of the curtain, and can't be seen when the curtain is opened or closed.

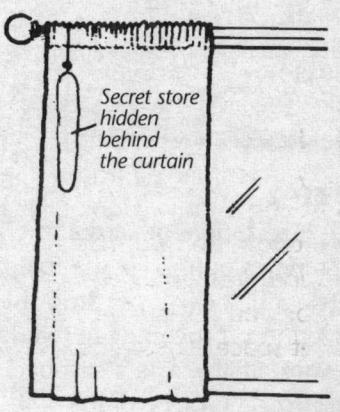

Secret store hidden behind the curtain

Top secret

Alarming idea

James Bond and other super sleuths moisten a strand of hair and press it across a door opening to find out if anyone has entered a room. This simple system works a treat, but to discourage nosey brothers or sisters you need a buzzer alarm. You may have already constructed something similar at school when studying electricity and circuits.

To make the buzzer alarm, you will need stiff card, aluminium foil, sticky tape, plastic-covered electrical wire, an electric buzzer or bell, batteries and battery holder. You'll find the electrical bits and bobs at some hardware shops and in most electrical or hobby shops.

Handy Mandy

Ask an adult to help strip the ends of the wire and to make the connections. The length of the wires depends on the distance between the 'trap' and the buzzer alarm and batteries.

STEP 1 ▶

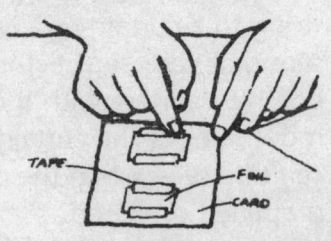

Cut a rectangle of card and two small rectangles of foil. Fix the foil to the card with sticky tape. Strip the covering off the ends of two lengths of wire. Sticky tape a stripped end of wire to each piece of foil.

Top secret

STEP 2 ▶

Strip the covering off the other end of the wires and connect one end to a battery, the other to the buzzer. Strip the covering off another length of wire and connect it between the buzzer and the other battery. Fold the card so that the foils make contact – the buzzer should sound.

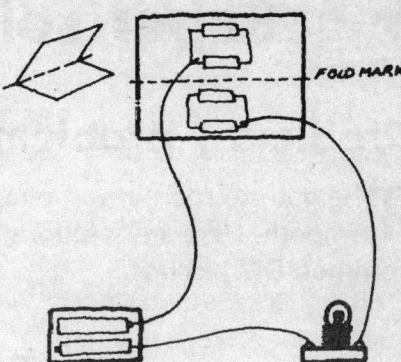

STEP 3 ▶

Place the card, partially folded so that the foils do not touch, under a rug near your door, desk or wardrobe. Conceal the wires and hide the batteries and buzzer out of sight. When someone steps on the card, the foils will make contact, the buzzer will ring, and someone will get the surprise of their life.

Handy Mandy

If the folded card collapses under the weight of the rug or through lots of use, prop it open with a small piece of washing-up sponge. To make the bell ring for a long time, fix double-sided tape along one edge of the rectangle of card.

# Super solutions

Problems, problems

The path to room revamping prowess is not always smooth. Here are solutions to a few of the more common DIY hiccups.

"I haven't any proper paint"

If time is short, the DIY shop is closed and the paint in the garage has hardened because the lid was left off, then improvise with other paints that you do have, such as acrylic or watercolour paints, which will do a perfectly reasonable job. The groovy, splatter-effect lampshade on the next page uses watercolour paint.

Super solutions

LAMPSHADE PARADE

For this excellent design, you need a plain, light-coloured, fabric lampshade, an old eye-drops container and some watercolour paints.

STEP 1 ▶

Lightly dampen the entire lampshade by wiping it with a well-dampened sponge or brush.

STEP 2 ▶

Mix the paint with some water in a small container, then suck up a small amount of the paint into the eye-dropper.

STEP 3 ▶

Release one drop gently onto the surface of the shade. Wait to see how far the paint spreads before positioning the next drop of paint. Repeat until you have created splatters all round the lampshade.

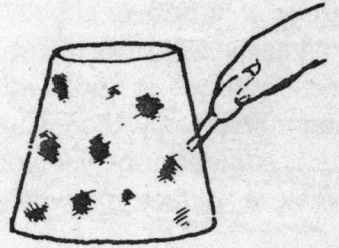

"I can't paint or paper my walls"

Okay, but surely you can have posters and pictures on your walls? Get an adult on side and ask him or her to knock in nails and hooks on which you can hang wallhangings and other decorations, or ask instead to fix things to your walls with sticky tack (easily removed) or double-sided tape (harder, but not impossible to remove).

Super solutions

"I'm not allowed to use varnish"

Because the fumes released when using varnish are strong, it is understandable that some parents might forbid its use, even when used indoors with plenty of ventilation or outdoors.

Instead of varnish, you can protect, seal and give a semi-glossy finish using a mixture of 1 part water with 1 part PVA glue. Apply the white mixture with a soft brush and watch it dry to a clear finish. When painting it over water-based paint, be very careful not to drag or scrape the brush across the painted surface. This will prevent the paint underneath smudging. A PVA-water finish is not water resistant, so only use it when there's no chance of the item getting wet.

"I don't have a work surface"   AAGRRH!

Join the queue, but here's an idea that might just work in your home. What you need is a piece of hardboard that is the same size as your desk or about 100 cm by 60 cm. Ask an adult or staff at the DIY store to cut it in half or into thirds. Join the sections together using wide, strong tape so that they fold and unfold easily. Store your portable, fold-out DIY work surface under or behind your bed and use it to protect whatever surface you work on!

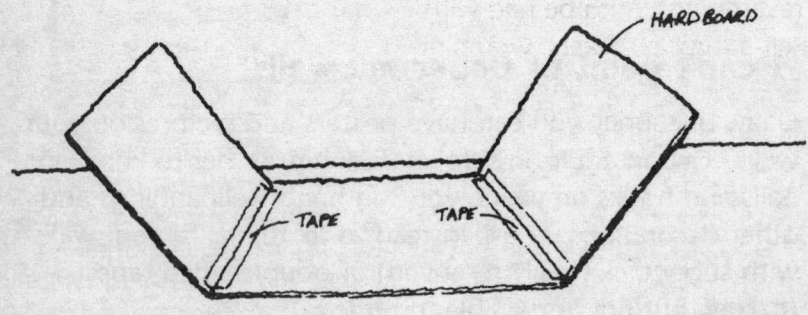

Super solutions

"All my furniture is brand new"

Keep a look out for cheap or free chairs, stools, small cabinets, picture frames and anything else in junk shops, on skips or in your great-aunt Martha's garden shed. It doesn't matter how sad, tatty or tasteless it is, you can turn it into a designer item. It often costs no more than the price of a single-hit cassette to get your hands on something that will let you express your creativity.

"Have you any no-mess projects?"

There are plenty of small revamping ideas that don't involve painting, gluing, sawing and hammering. The first place to look for no-mess decorating materials are stationery shops and craft/fabric shops. There's no end of revamping fun to be had with self-adhesive stickers, wrapping and tissue paper, fabric remnants, ribbons, threads and fancy cords and braids. Here's one idea using a mirror or picture frame and self-adhesive stickers to get you started.

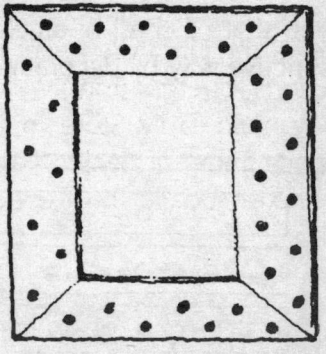

A pack of self-adhesive silver dots can be carefully applied to a smooth, clean photo or mirror frame to look like the rivets you find on steel or iron girders. This pocket money project is mess-free and very now!

Super solutions

Two's company

Sharing a room with an older or younger sibling is never easy. It is even more stressful when you both try to express your different personalities in the way you decorate your spaces. But before you start dreaming up revamping ideas perhaps the two of you should sign a "Sharer's Charter" in which you agree to talk about ideas first and accept that compromises will be necessary.

Here are a few revamping ideas that will let you mark your territory without the threat of all-out sibling civil war.

Top drawer

If you share a chest of drawers, brighten them up in your own distinctive way by decorating the drawer fronts and knobs.

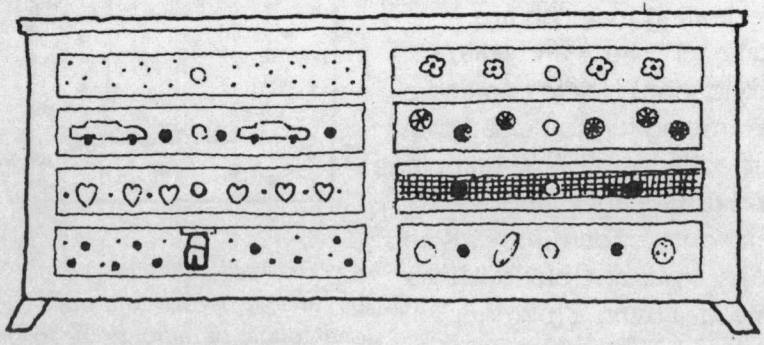

Here are eight decorating ideas to inspire you. Ideally, you and your sibling would select just one theme each.

Super solutions

The great divide

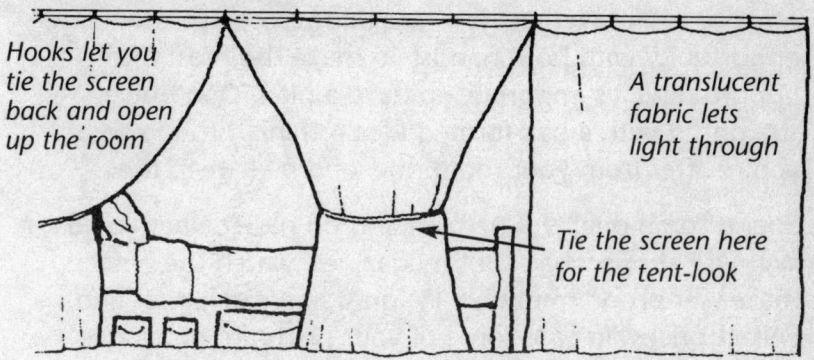

Hooks let you tie the screen back and open up the room

A translucent fabric lets light through

Tie the screen here for the tent-look

If your room is on the large side and both you and your sibling have your own desk and storage spaces, all you might be lacking is privacy. This pull-back curtain, which separates 'your half' from 'their half', could be just the solution you're seeking.

The fabric curtain can be suspended from hooks in the ceiling, from a pole that runs from one wall to another, or even along a curtain track. Because it is a major job, you'll need the permission and the assistance of an adult.

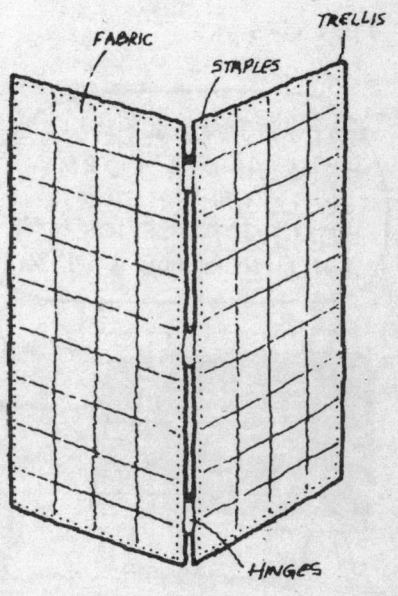

If you can't divide the room, then make a folding screen using two panels of wooden garden trellis joined with hinges and covered with a light fabric. The fabric is fixed to the frame of the trellis using a staple gun.

Super solutions

"My parents want to redecorate my room"

A major room overhaul is a rare thing, so grasp the opportunity with both hands! To make the most of this opportunity, it's important to have a plan. Don't dive straight in with a half-formed idea – think through what you're after from your room now and next year, too.

Spend some quality time planning on paper what you'd like. Visit shops, check out magazines, watch the endless makeover programmes on TV, grab free catalogues and collect prices. In case some of your plans are unfeasible – a jacuzzi and a full-sized snooker table may be a tad too ambitious – have back-up plans at the ready. The more information you have, the more impressive your case will be when you get round to discussing it with your parents. Be prepared for a bit of compromise and bargaining and understand that costs quickly mount.

Super solutions

"Help, I put my rollerblades under my bed and now I can't find them"

This is what happens when you just keep throwing stuff under your bed. What you need to do is organise your under-bed storage using boxes that can be easily accessed. It's when storage is hard to get at that you don't use it.

Get hold of several strong cardboard boxes and cut them down to a height that fits neatly under your bed. Decorate them by covering the front (or all sides) with wrapping paper or cut-outs from magazines. Make two holes in the front and thread through strong cord. Attach a 'toy' or label to the cord to indicate the contents of the box and firmly knot the ends of the cord inside the box.

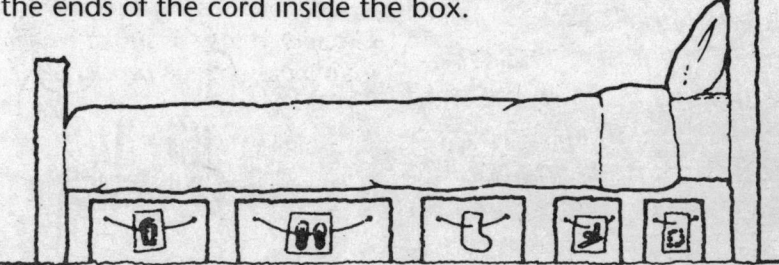

Choose boxes to suit the contents – bigger boxes for large items, smaller ones for tiny treasures. To find what you want it's simply a matter of picking the right box, pulling on the cord and dragging out the box.

Super solutions

Clutter killers

Mess, mess, mess! We can all handle the odd complaint from a parent about the state of our room, but when it starts to mushroom into forfeiting trips and treats because of the bomb site that is your bedroom, you know you've got problems. An even better test is when all the mess starts to really get you down. So what can be done about it?

No-tip tips

1 Several pinboards can hold an enormous amount of paper that would otherwise be scattered over your desk and on the floor. But before pinning something to a pinboard, ask yourself this – do I really need last Christmas's wish-list?

2 Bulldog clips fixed to a length of wood, to the end of a shelf or inside a wardrobe (see page 49) are perfect hold-alls for all sorts of gear.

3 Empty baked bean tins make great pencil holders – you'd pay heaps in the shops for purpose-made, shiny, metallic tins. Ask an adult to fold over the opened end with pliers to get rid of the sharp, jagged edge, then remove the label and glue by soaking the tin in hot water. AAGRRH!

Bind four tins together with coloured tape or strong twine to make a mega pencil holder.

Super solutions

4 To store your magazines, all you need to do is eat your breakfast cereal! Take an empty cereal box, tape the base to strengthen it and then trim the top, as shown, to make a magazine file.

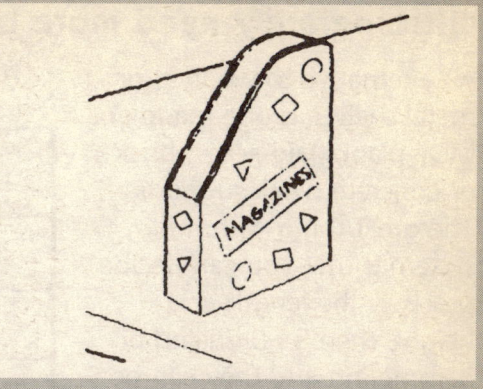

Once decorated with paper or sticky-back plastic and other trimmings, you'd never know that a cereal box was lurking beneath.

5 Obtain a number of jars that have screw-on lids, and soak them in hot water to remove labels and glue. Make one or two holes in each lid with a large nail and hammer. Glue the top of the lids to the underside of a wooden shelf with strong glue, then securely fix with screws. (Ask an adult to do this for you.) Screw on the jars and you have see-through storage for paperclips, rubber bands, hair clips or even your coin collection!

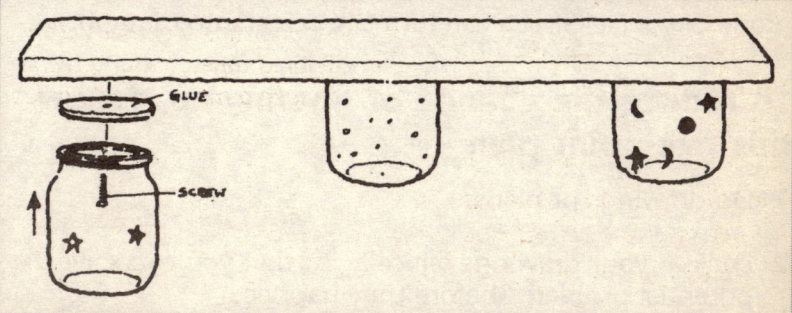

Decorate the jars with self-adhesive dots and stars that still let you see the contents.

Super solutions

"I desperately need more bookshelves"

An alternative to wooden or metal shelves is one made of MDF planks laid across brick or concrete block supports. The great thing with this system is that you can decide precisely the length and height, there's no drilling or hammering and they can be easily dismantled or moved. In their raw state, they are not the most attractive, but the MDF and bricks can be painted or sprayed.

"I mucked up one of my DIY projects"

This happens to everyone, so don't get all down about it. What you have to do is work out if it can be made good or whether you should undo what you've done and start again. But whatever you do, don't just chuck it and all your effort away. You'll learn much more trying to right it and you'll be dead proud of yourself if you can turn DIY defeat into triumph.

To reduce the chance of goofing-up, follow this five-point plan –

1 Do drawings or plans.

2 Look at your drawings critically, so that you can solve potential problems before they happen.

3 Give yourself plenty of time. Rome and your bedroom can't be built in a day!

Super solutions

4 If you get stuck, ask an adult for help.

5 Make sure you've got everything you need before you start. You may not be able to get your hands on a particular item that could jeopardise your whole plan.

"My parents think my ideas will be too hard to do"

There's a simple answer to this – KISS! Kiss stands for 'Keep it simple, stupid' and it is the motto used by people who create advertising campaigns. Perhaps it would be good to remember KISS when coming up with revamping ideas. If you can keep your ideas simple, it will be easier to do a really great job and to finish it. Make your ideas too ambitious and you may run out of steam halfway through.

 # Want to know more?

Now that you're a first-class room revamper, you'll always be on the look out for new ideas, novel materials and ways in which you can improve your techniques and move onto more complicated jobs.

Magazines and newspapers

There are scores of interior design magazines on the shelves of newsagents and many newspapers come with home design supplements or have a regular design or DIY contributor. Sadly, magazines and newspapers do not come cheap, so ask parents and relatives to hand their copies onto you when they have finished. If the magazines and newspapers are no longer wanted, cut out items of interest and paste them into a scrapbook.

Hardware and DIY shops

If your folks are off to a home improvements store, go with them and use the time to check out prices, sizes and types of products available on the shelves. Many DIY shops produce small how-to leaflets, and while some are aimed at the committed DIY specialist, many show basic DIY techniques. These leaflets are usually free.

Craft shops

Small craft or fabric shops are usually manned by very experienced staff who know everything there is to know about crafty things. If you are buying something from their shop and they are not busy, the staff will be happy to help solve a crafty, revamp problem.

Want to know more?

Books

There are few revamp-your-room books aimed at kids, which is why we wrote this book for you! Most of these titles are aimed at adults, but they are worth borrowing from the library.

Art Attack
Neil Buchanan (Dorling Kindersley)
Buchanan's ideas for things practical and decorative are fun and wacky. A great book if you're looking for colourful inspiration.

Environment Friendly Home Hints
Family Circle (Fairfax Press)
This isn't strictly a room makeover guide, but it does include lots of interesting tips on recycling, re-using old containers and indoor gardening.

Transform Your Home In A Weekend
Stewart and Sally Walton (Sebastian Kelly Press/Anness Publishing Ltd)
Over 100 makeover projects in a big, bright and breezy book. Some are out of your league, others will be right up your street.

The Thrifty Decorator
Jocasta Innes (Conran Octopus)
Jocasta is one of the very top interior designers and her ideas on revamping on a budget are fascinating.

The Big Blue Craft Book
(Aceville Publications)
This is a directory of all sorts of craft shops and suppliers around Britain. A money-saving tip – look in bargain bookshops for a bargain-priced copy of last year's edition.

Want to know more?

Revamping ideas on the Net

http://www.craftfair.co.uk/
This is one groovy web site, chock-full of information and useful contacts for all your craft materials and magazines. Particularly worth looking at is the site's learning zone where craft ideas and techniques are explained.

http://www.nhptv.org/kn/vs/artlkd2.sht
Arts and crafts just for kids at this fun web site. Learn how to make your own paper and use new painting techniques to transform objects around your room.

http://homearts.com/shelter
A very interesting interior design web site. Although designed with adults in mind, there are plenty of tips and quite a few activities which may interest you.

http://www.schoolworld.asn.au/resource/art.html
For the more arty amongst you, this Australian web site is a great first port of call for some excellent links to arts resources on the Internet.

http://www.wyomingcompanion.com/janacraft/links2.htm
JanaCraft's collection of craft and interior design links is one of the very best around. The rest of this web site isn't bad either!

http://www.craft.com/
Everything to do with crafts and lots of free patterns and projects for things to make.

Glossary

Aagrrh! – a *Room Makeover* catchphrase that means 'get an adult to help you'.

Acrylic paint – a quick-drying, water-based paint. Clean brushes with water and detergent.

Artificial turf – fake grass made from plastic.

Blackboard paint – a special matt black paint that can be written on with chalk.

Bradawl – most often used to make a 'starter' hole for screws in softwood or MDF.

Bulldog clip – strong, spring-loaded clip.

Card – a smooth paper product as used to make cereal packets.

Carpet squares – carpet-like floor covering.

Coats of paint – each time you cover a surface with a layer of paint, you are applying a coat of paint. Each coat must be dry before the next is applied.

Coping saw – a saw with a thin blade and a square frame used for cutting irregular shapes out of wood and board.

Cork tiles – squares or strips of cork, a little thicker than corrugated card. Can be cut with a Stanley knife.

Corrugated card – a strong card that consists of a wavy layer sandwiched between two flat layers of card.

Craft glue – sometimes known as white or an all-purpose glue, it dries clear and can be used for paper, card, wood, leather and some plastics.

Crêpe paper – thin yet strong paper with a 'wrinkled' surface.

Cup hook – metal or plastic-covered open hook with a screw-threaded end.

DIY – 'Do It Yourself' describes a way of making things and also large hardware shops.

Dowelling – rods of wood with a round cross-section. Curtains can be hung from dowelling.

Eco-friendly – materials and activities that cause little or no harm to the environment, wildlife and humans.
Emulsion paint – there are internal and external types of this water-based, quick-drying paint. More than one coat is needed to create an even and hard-wearing finish. Clean brushes with water and detergent.
Enamel paint – a non-toxic paint for metal and wood (especially furniture and children's toys). It is expensive, so best for only small jobs. Wash brush in white spirit. *AAGRRH!*
Face mask – a mask made from fibres that is worn over the nose and mouth to prevent dust and fumes from damaging throat and lungs.
Felt – a soft fabric that does not fray when cut.
Fittings – the bits that are attached to a piece of furniture or a room. Drawer and door handles, door knockers and hooks are all fittings.
G-clamp – an adjustable metal tool in the shape of a G that grips one or more items to hold them steady.
Gloss – describes any surface with a shiny finish.
Gloss paint – sometimes called a topcoat or a one-coat paint, this oil-based paint dries slowly to a shiny finish. Good for wood and metal.
Glue gun – a special applicator that allows easily-controlled amounts of glue to go exactly where they are wanted.
Goo-goo eyes – fake plastic eyes with 'wobbly' black centres.
Hacksaw – a saw used for cutting metal or hard plastics. A small hacksaw is quite easy to use.
Hardboard – a manufactured, thin board made of wood fibres.
Hardwood – a dark-coloured wood from deciduous trees like oak. Hardwoods are tough, long-lasting and quite expensive.
Join – this means butting items together and is also the 'place' where surfaces meet.

Glossary

Luminous paint – this paint glows in the dark.
Masking tape – an easily-removed sticky tape that is used to protect or 'mask off' areas of a surface when painting.
Matt – a non-shiny finish.
MDF – medium density fibre-board is a man-made material that is used in place of wood. It's relatively cheap and can be easily cut, drilled and finished.
Metal paint – suitable to cover, colour and protect a bare metal surface.
Metallic paint – creates a finish that resembles a shiny metal, even though the material painted may be plastic, wood, MDF, glass or card.
Mosaic tiles – small ceramic or mirror tiles used in numbers to make up a picture or pattern.
Nails – sharp, pointed fixings that are driven into place with a hammer.
Painting sheets – large pieces of cloth or plastic thrown over furniture and flooring while you are painting. Old bedsheets make good painting sheets.
Panel pin – a thin nail with a small head used to join pieces of wood and MDF.
Pliers – a gripping tool for holding fiddly items, bending wire and for removing or tightening bolts and screw-in fittings.
Polystyrene – a lightweight and soft man-made material that is easily cut and pierced. Swim kickboards are made of polystyrene.
Power tool – any tool that is powered by electricity.
PVA glue – water-soluble glue that forms a reasonably strong bond. PVA glue works on most materials, except plastics.
Right angle – each corner of a square or rectangle is a right angle because the two sides meet at 90 degrees. A try square tool can be used to make perfect right-angle joins.
Sandpaper – an abrasive paper used for smoothing wood and other surfaces.
Screws – threaded fixings that provide a strong join between two surfaces.
Self-adhesive hook – a plastic hook backed with a

Glossary

sticky pad that can be fixed to a smooth surface. Not as strong as screwed-in hooks.

Softwoods – wood from coniferous tress like pine or spruce. It is light-coloured and less hardwearing than hardwoods.

Spray paint – a gas (called a propellant) forces a fine spray of paint out of the metal container when the nozzle is pressed. It provides an even coverage without any brush marks.

Stanley knife – a strong cutting knife with a large, replaceable and very sharp blade.

Staple gun – a tool that releases and drives large pointed staples into wood or MDF.

Stencil – a reuseable piece of thin card, plastic or wood that is cut into a shape. Lay the stencil on a surface and paint around and over it to reproduce the desired shape.

Stick glue – a solid glue containing a lipstick-like container that is used for paper and card.

Sticky-back plastic – a thin layer of plastic that has a sticky backing.

Sticky tack – sold under many different names, this soft material is used to fix posters to a wall. It is easily removed.

Suction hook – a plastic hook that is held in place with a suction pad.

Sugarpaper – a thick craft paper.

Tack – a nail that can fix fabric to wood.

Template – a card or paper cut out of a shape that can be drawn and painted around.

Translucent – a material that lets some but not all light through. Lampshades are often translucent.

Twine – a rough, strong string that is often used in gardening.

Varnish – a liquid that is brushed or sprayed on to provide a protective coating to wood and other materials.

Index

Aagrrh! 17
alarm 104-105

backstitch 24
beads 11, 32
bed decoration 55
blackboard 74-75
blanket stitch 24
bookends 62
book, secret space in 100-101
bradawl 18, 21

card 23
carpet squares 50-51
CD
    screen 68
    whiteboard 69
clipboard 74-75
Computer crazy 56-69
computer frame 60-61
copy holder 65
cork tiles 11
corrugated card 23
craft glue, white 25
craft knife 18, 22
curtains (*see also* wallhangings and screens)
    recycling 10
    rods 55
cutting 22

dartboard 54
decorating themes 14-15, 70
doorstop 65, 79, 96
double-sided tape 26, 107
dowelling 23
draught excluder 79

drawer
    compartment 102
    decorating 110
drawing pins 64
duvet 40, 47

eco-friendly 71

fabric 10, 24, 28-29
fake hand 92-93
floor decoration 50-51
fried egg cushion 13
Fright night 86-97

glue 25
Great outdoors, indoors 70-85

Halloween bargains 87
hammer 18, 22
hand drill 18
hardboard 11, 23
hole punch 18
hook rack 49

kit box 48-49

lampshades 32-33, 54, 76-77, 107

manacles 97
masking tape 26, 51
materials 23-27
    no-mess 109
Material world, it's a 28-41
MDF 11, 23
mirror frames 38-39
mobile 84
mouse 67
mouse mat 66

125

Index

packing tape 26
paint 27, 43
    chips 43
    glow-in-the dark 91
    watercolour 106
paintbrushes 18
paper 23
papier mâché 76-77
pebbles 85
pen holder 64
pinboard 36-37, 54
planning 112, 116-117
plant containers 80, 85
'plaster' cast 85
pliers 19, 21
privacy 98, 99
PVA glue 25, 108

recycling 10-11
    bin 78
    locating 12-13, 29, 57, 109
    storing 11
research 42-43
ribbon basket 40
ribbons 10
room
    decorating themes 14-15, 70, 117
    dividers 111
    problems 6, 8-9
    sharing 110-111
rubbish bin 78
rug 41

safety 17
sand, coloured 84
saws 19
scissors 19
screens 41, 55, 68, 111
screwdriver 19
shelves 63, 116
sock container 48
softwoods 11, 23
sound recordings 71, 97
spider web 94
Sport, designs on 42-55
Stanley knife 20, 22
staple gun 20
steel rule 20
stencils 85
sticky tack 26, 107
sticky tape 26
stool
    fur-covered 34-35
    paper-covered 63
storage ideas 40, 48-49, 103, 113, 114-115
sugarpaper 23
Super solutions 106-117

tape measure 20
thread 11
tie-dye 82-83
tools 18-21
Top secret 98-105
trainer container 48
turf, artificial 50-51

varnish 108
vase 81

wall decoration 52-53
wallhangings 41, 46, 55, 90-91
warning signs 95, 99
wood 23
work area 16, 108
work clothes 17

super.activ

0 340 773294	Acting	£3.99	☐
0 340 764686	Athletics	£3.99	☐
0 340 791578	Basketball	£3.99	☐
0 340 791535	Cartooning	£3.99	☐
0 340 791624	Chess	£3.99	☐
0 340 791586	Computers Unlimited	£3.99	☐
0 340 79156X	Cricket	£3.99	☐
0 340 791594	Drawing	£3.99	☐
0 340 791632	Film-making	£3.99	☐
0 340 791675	Fishing	£3.99	☐
0 340 791519	Football	£3.99	☐
0 340 76466X	Golf	£3.99	☐
0 340 778970	Gymnastics	£3.99	☐
0 340 739819	Ice Skating	£3.99	☐
0 340 791527	In-line Skating	£3.99	☐
0 340 764678	Juggling	£3.99	☐
0 340 749504	Karate	£3.99	☐
0 340 791640	The Internet	£3.99	☐
0 340 791683	Memory Workout	£3.99	☐
0 340 736283	Pop Music	£3.99	☐
0 340 791551	Riding	£3.99	☐
0 340 791659	Rugby	£3.99	☐
0 340 791608	Skateboarding	£3.99	☐
0 340 791667	Snowboarding	£3.99	☐
0 340 791616	Swimming	£3.99	☐
0 340 764465	Tennis	£3.99	☐
0 340 773332	Writing	£3.99	☐
0 340 784822	Your Own Chat Room	£3.99	☐
0 340 791543	Your Own Website	£3.99	☐

ORDER FORM

Books in the **super.activ** series are available at your local bookshops, or can be ordered direct from the publisher.
A complete list of titles is given on the previous page. Just tick the titles you want and complete the details below. Prices and availability are subject to change without prior notice.

Please enclose a cheque or postal order made payable to Bookpoint Ltd, and send to: Hodder Children's Books, Cash Sales Dept, Bookpoint, 39 Milton Park, Abingdon, Oxon OX14 4TD.
Email address: orders@bookpoint.co.uk.

If you would prefer to pay by credit card, our call centre team would be delighted to take your order by telephone.
Our direct line is 01235 400414 (lines open 9.00 am – 6.00 pm, Monday to Saturday; 24-hour message answering service).
Alternatively you can send a fax on 01235 400454.

Title .... First name .... Surname ....

Address ....

....

....

Daytime tel .... Postcode ....

If you would prefer to post a credit card order, please complete the following.

Please debit my Visa/Access/Diner's Card/American Express (delete as applicable) card number:

Signature ....

Expiry Date ....

If you would NOT like to receive further
information on our products, please tick ☐ .